P9-DBL-355

A PERSONAL STAND

VILLARD

NEW YORK

A PERSONAL STAND

Observations and Opinions
from a Freethinking Roughneck

TRACE ADKINS

with Keith and Kent Zimmerman

Copyright © 2007 by Trace Adkins

All rights reserved.

Published in the United States by Villard Books,
an imprint of The Random House Publishing Group,
a division of Random House, Inc., New York.

VILLARD and "V" Circled Design are registered
trademarks of Random House, Inc.

Grateful acknowledgment is made to Universal Music Publishing Group
and Sawng Cumpny (ASCAP) for permission to reprint lyrics from
"Welcome to Hell" by Trace Adkins and Bobby Terry, copyright © 2003
by Almo Music Corporation, Jill's Mad Money Music. All rights for Jill's
Mad Money Music administered by Almo Music Corporation/ASCAP.
Copyright © Sawng Cumpny (ASCAP). All rights reserved.
Used by permission.

Adkins, Trace.
A personal stand: observations and opinions from a freethinking
roughneck / Trace Adkins; with Keith and Kent Zimmerman.
p.   cm.
ISBN 978-0-345-49933-2
1. Adkins, Trace.   2. Country musicians—Unites States—Biography.
I. Zimmerman, Kent.   II. Zimmerman, Keith.   III. Title.
ML420.A215A3   2007
782.421642092—dc22   2007029981
[B]

Printed in the United States of America on acid-free paper

www.villard.com

2 4 6 8 9 7 5 3 1

FIRST EDITION

Book design by Barbara M. Bachman

CONTENTS

CALLIN' 'EM LIKE I SEE 'EM

WRITING THIS BOOK HAS BEEN AN INCREDIBLE LEARNING experience, and what I have learned is that I do not particularly like writing books. However, I have been urged by several people to do this and I agreed to, so here it goes . . .

I stand for personal responsibility and against anything that undermines it. So much of what I see in our country today represents a hell-bent flight from responsibility to victimhood. From acting on one's convictions to going along just to get along. From making decisions based on moral principles to taking the easy way out. That's not what the United States of America is about, and that's not the legacy our children should inherit.

In this book I'll refer to my life experiences, but it's not the next celebrity confession. I'll be talking about the state of this country as I've seen it from my boyhood in small-town Louisiana to these days of headlining concerts across our land. I'll talk about my journey from being an oilfield hand with few responsibilities (except an honest day's work), to being a father of five daughters and the president of a small corporation.

I'll be touching on some of today's hot-button issues: trade unionism, energy and the environment, Republicans and Democrats, illegal immigration, the war on terrorism, and freedom of speech. I'll also have some things to say about blame games and pity parties, fatherhood and the personal conflict I face from not having had a real job since I became a full-time musician.

With me, what you see is what you get. I don't put on airs, I don't pull punches, and most important, I don't take myself too seriously. I'm not in the loop inside the Beltway, and I don't claim to have the scoop on anything.

I just call 'em like I see 'em.

Chapter One

THE DAY THERE WERE NO PLANES

I T'S A DAMN GOOD THING I WASN'T THE PRESIDENT AFTER
9/11 because I would have . . . let's not go there yet. But there are
defining moments for every generation. The events of 9/11 were
my generation's defining moment, so we'll start there.

On the morning of September 11, 2001, I was sitting in my
garage watching TV like I usually do. It's my morning ritual.
When I'm home and off the road, I go out into the garage for a
cigarette—because I can't smoke in the house, which is cool. On
that fateful day I dutifully retreated to the garage with my big mug
of black coffee. I watched the Weather Channel to see if I was
going to bother going outside, and then I flipped over to Fox
News to start my day.

I was watching live news coverage when the second plane hit.
As the shocking facts came together and it was apparent that the
Twin Towers were being attacked by terrorists, I felt a deep rage
building up to a boiling point. I was seething inside over the fact
that someone would hate Americans so much as to commit such a
heinous crime.

Then, like so many Americans, I needed to deal with the 9/11
tragedy on my own home front.

By lunchtime, after I had gotten over the initial shock of what had happened, I focused my attention on Mackenzie, my three-year-old little girl. I knew that what had just happened didn't mean anything to her and that she had no idea what was going on.

At the time we lived just south of Nashville International Airport, far enough from it that the noise didn't ever bother us, but still within its busy flight patterns. When the winds came out of the north, the aircraft flew high over our house on their approach to BNA. My little girl loved to watch the planes come over.

So that day, I took her outside and went to the front yard where we could both clearly see the sky. We lay down on our backs on a grassy knoll with the noonday sun beating down on our faces from a completely cloudless canopy.

I leaned over to Mackenzie and said, "Let's see how many airplanes we can count."

She was excited. So we waited. And we waited. There were no planes. *No planes at all.* Now, you can't keep a three-year-old's interest for very long.

"There are no planes," she finally said and jumped up. "C'mon, Daddy, let's go do something else."

I held Mackenzie in my arms for a little while. Then I said to her, "Look at me, sweetheart, and I want you to remember this. There was a day when Daddy took you outside to see the planes and there were no planes flying anywhere in the sky. No planes."

"Why, Daddy?"

"Today the president said, 'No one can fly planes today,' so there are none. Today's the only day this will happen. You will never see this again. I want you to remember what Daddy showed you on the day there were no planes."

That was the only way I could impress upon a three-year-old the importance of that sad and terrible time.

Chapter Two

CIVIS AMERICANIS

THE 9/11 ATTACKS REALLY MADE ME THINK ABOUT MY children and their future twenty years from now. Would they be free to pursue their everyday hopes and dreams without fear, without worrying that some evil person was going to plant a bomb in the mall or blow up an airliner? Were my children going to have to exist in a country riddled with fear?

Having to live in constant dread is like being forced back to the caveman days when every time you stepped outside, you had to worry about whether a saber-toothed tiger was going to eat you. Before 9/11, I thought civilization had progressed beyond that point. Yet with all this pent-up religious tension, I'm not so sure anymore.

Had I been president in September 2001, once we ascertained that Islamic fundamentalists had committed this atrocity I would have demanded a conference call with every Arab leader in the world:

"Listen. If this is the first salvo, the first shot, and if this is going to continue, then let it be known today that it *will not* continue for very long. We have the firepower to end this, and we're willing to use it. My children and my grandchildren will not live in fear for the rest of their lives because that's not living. That's just existing."

I would have put it all on the line.

"I'm warning you folks right now, I'm willing to end it all. I will incinerate this rock starting with Afghanistan, and I mean it. If you're not going to get with the terrorist eradication program and get your shit together, and if you permit this stuff to go on in your own countries, by God, I will end this now. We will all go to our maker and we'll let Him decide who was right." (It would have been at that moment, hopefully, that some sensible person in my administration would have dropped a horse tranquilizer in my coffee.)

The United States didn't ask to be the security force for the entire globe. That role is being forced upon us because nobody else will stand up against the evil in this world. That's right. We're being *forcibly* put in a position of responsibility because of the apathy and negligence of other world leaders. We didn't ask to be the World Cop, and the American people don't want that job any more than anybody else does.

I used to watch the television series *West Wing*. I loved that show, and in the early days, although I'm a conservative, I never missed an episode and recorded the ones that I did miss. I dug it. It didn't make me question any of my political affiliations; I enjoyed the show and kept it in perspective. My favorite episode was when Martin Sheen, as President Jed Bartlett, equated freedom and our way of life to the time of the Romans, when a Roman citizen could travel anywhere in the known world. And if ever he was confronted with potential trouble or danger all he had to say was, "*Civis Romanis*. I am a Roman citizen."

So great and universal was the fear of retribution from Rome that any Roman citizen could walk anywhere in the known world cloaked in those words and immediately know that a given situation would be defused. He had the protection of the Roman Empire. Nobody messed with that. President Bartlett was saying on *West Wing* that that is the way it should be for American citizens today. We should be able to travel the globe and say, "*Civis Americanis.* I am an American citizen."

We are the most powerful nation on the globe, and by God, that comes with benefits! I'm not saying we should travel in arrogance or cockiness and strut through downtown Baghdad expecting people to part like the Red Sea. All I ask is for the rest of the world to treat Americans with respect so we don't have to kill you. (Oh, lighten up! I'm just kidding.)

Contrary to what some people on the left might intimate, Americans are not indiscriminate killers. We have to be provoked to strike. It's like that famous World War II quote attributed to Admiral Isoroku Yamamoto after the Japanese attacked Pearl Harbor: "I fear all we have done is awaken a sleeping giant and fill him with a terrible resolve." Now whether or not he actually uttered those exact words, he surely knew what the Japanese had just done. They'd committed a military blunder. They had just opened up a big can of whup-ass. Retribution was coming, and he knew it.

As Americans, we won't mess with you or bother you, but just know that when you kill innocent Americans, you've opened that can and we're gonna come for you. Like the Romans did. For every one of our people you kill, we're going to kill a thousand of yours. And if you think you have the Monopoly money to stay in the game, then keep on and know that every time you land on Boardwalk, we're gonna collect.

I APPEARED ON BILL MAHER'S show *Politically Incorrect* on ABC exactly one month after the World Trade Center destruction. I was booked along with Julian Epstein, a former chief Democratic counsel for the House Judiciary Committee; an environmental writer named Bjorn Lomborg; and Elayne Boosler, a comedienne who had been active with the Democratic Party and the National Organization for Women. All through the show, those three guests were preaching this peaceful message of tolerance toward Muslims. Bill was having none of it and neither was I.

Maher quoted a *New York Times Magazine* article by journalist Andrew Sullivan saying that 9/11 was part of a religious war being waged by Osama bin Laden and extremist Muslims and that "the religious dimension of this conflict . . . represents a part of Islam that certainly cannot be denied or ignored." Maher went on to quote a few intolerant verses from the Koran, including "kill them where you find them," referring to all of us so-called "infidels."

I was surprised at the reaction of the other three panelists. Boosler was quick to point out that such verses could be found in the Bible. Epstein emphasized that 9/11 should not ignite a war against Islam, and mentioned that some of the Christians who bombed Sarajevo during the Bosnian conflict were also driven by the same kind of extremism. The tree-hugging author mentioned the Crusades from the twelfth and thirteenth centuries and suggested that we help modernize and educate Islamic people so they wouldn't buy into bin Laden's beliefs. All three felt that education would help stem this tidal wave of extremism and terrorism.

Horse dookey! (Writing about this without cussing is hard.)

I thought to myself, Is this what the average American is thinking today, October 11, 2001? Hell no! I saw a full-scale guilt-trip pity party going on. I couldn't believe these people were wringing their hands and talking this way one month after 2,973 Americans were murdered by Islamic terrorists. They were trying to intellectualize the reasons why terrorists blew up our World Trade Center and they were completely missing the point.

"I think we're all in a huge state of denial here. I really do," I said to the panel. "I think everybody in America that's trying to find some kind of negotiated way through this whole maze is just fooling themselves. They're putting off the inevitable.

"This is going to come down to a scrap, and it's going to be big and we're going to have to settle this thing once and for all. We're gonna have to end this thing. We're going to have to fight it out till it's over and until they don't do this anymore. We're going to have to go into Afghanistan and take care of this, and if Pakistan doesn't like it, we thump their ass, too. That's what we have to do. It's inevitable."

Bill Maher cracked a smile on camera. He doesn't know too many backwoods boys like me.

The other guests were shocked at my gung-ho position. Epstein pointed out that "a revulsion against modernism" came about because poor Muslims were forced to live under cruel dictatorships and enormous poverty.

I tried to get back to the bottom line: These people hate us and they want to eradicate us.

"I for one," I spoke up, "don't care what it's about. I don't care if it's about religion or politics or economics or what it is. I know that they want to kill us and we have to kill them to stop it from happening. I don't care what the reason is. They want to kill us! That's all they care about. If we don't kill them, we might as well just give up and say, 'Okay, come live over here with us.'"

Then we went to a commercial break. That was when the best stuff always happened on that show; unfortunately, the current HBO version doesn't go to commercial spots.

After we went to a commercial break, Mr. Epstein, the brainiac lawyer, leaned across the table to me and said, "Man, you are really off the deep end and barbaric about this."

I leaned across the table to him and said, "You're damn right I am! And of all people, you should be, too. Your last name is Epstein, for God's sake. Those anti-Semitic monsters hate you a lot worse than they do me! They might not give a shit about me, but they wouldn't even waste time talking to you. They'll just kill you. All they have to see is your last name and you're a dead man. And you're going to sit here and try to figure out why they're doing all this stuff? Give me a break, man. Get on board the train, hoss. We're pulling out, and we're going to kill these expletive deleteds."

Epstein just sat back in his chair. I really got in his face. The lesson was, don't patronize me. That kind of attitude sucks, so don't go there. And don't insult me by thinking I'm not serious about what I say.

I guess at first he really thought I was just trying to be a redneck and say all these outlandish things simply for the television shock value. Then as he listened to me a little while longer, I think he realized I truly meant what I said. And it seemed to freak him out even more that I honestly felt that way. Maybe he just couldn't believe it. Yet on the other hand, I don't understand people in this country who don't feel the same anger that I feel.

Looking back, I stand by those words I uttered one month after the invasion. I still believe the only way to fight Islamic terrorism is to crack skulls. After eight years, Al-Qaeda is not going to go away through kindness, education, and tolerance. We need to flush them out of their caves and kill them. Then stream that footage live over the Internet.

I think that message will be pretty clear . . .

Civis Americanis!

Chapter Three

I CAME HERE TO LIVE: GROWING UP IN SAREPTA

. . .

I GREW UP IN A TOWN WHERE TOUGH WAS A CIGARETTE AND A SOUPED-UP CAR ON A COUNTY ROAD.

—*"I Came Here to Live"*
from *Dangerous Man*

GREW UP IN SAREPTA, LOUISIANA. POPULATION 924. Three years ago, they finally replaced the flashing red and yellow light with a brand-new traffic signal at the intersection of Highway 371 and Highway 2. Sarepta is located about forty miles northeast of Shreveport and ten miles south of the Arkansas line. The next-closest town is Springhill, population 5,000, seven miles north up Highway 371 (as a matter of fact, I was born in the hospital there). Sarepta is a "dry" town, so to this day, you still have to drive to Springhill to buy any alcohol.

Geographically and culturally, Louisiana can be cut up into three different slices. The northwest corner of the state is a North Texas–type environment where the economy is based on oil, timber, and cattle. Northeast Louisiana is river bottom, a lot like Mississippi and southeastern Arkansas, with lots of farming and agri-culture. Southern Louisiana is Cajun-influenced, with cities like New Orleans, New Iberia, Lafayette, Lake Charles, and Baton Rouge. (Other Louisiana natives may disagree, but don't pay any attention to them.)

I grew up solid working-class stock. There were about five churches in our one little-bitty town. A Church of Christ, three Southern Baptist churches, and a Methodist church. My mama, Peggy, and all her sisters sang in the Baptist choir. My daddy, Aaron Adkins, retired in 2007 from International Paper Company after forty-something years working at the corrugating plant making cardboard. He mostly worked the swing shift. I don't know how he survived switching back and forth between those grave-yard, evening, and daytime hours.

"Never wake Daddy up," my mama used to warn us kids. "Especially when he's working graveyards." You didn't want to hear that bedroom door open at noon because if you did, that meant somebody was fixin' to get their ass tanned.

I was born on January 13, 1962, the oldest of three brothers. My younger brother, Clay, joined me in 1965 and is still my best friend. Then the family mascot (the baby is almost always the family mascot), Scott, completed our family unit in 1972.

I had a Norman Rockwell–style Southern childhood in small-town America. My paternal grandparents lived about a mile and a half from my home, while the maternal pair lived about three miles away. We were always there for each other in our peaceful little God-fearing town. It felt secure to be a kid with both sets of grandparents and lots of kinfolk close by whenever I needed them.

My Aunt Ruth owned and operated a general store in town. She sold a little of everything. You could buy boots, bullets, and baloney. The place had gas pumps out front where I'd pull up on my minibike, fill the gas tank for a quarter, and then go ride all over creation for a whole week. Back then we didn't ride around Sarepta wearing fancy helmets or knee pads or elbow pads. We rode commando, and those of us who lived have the scars to prove it.

I was a fairly well-behaved kid who didn't get into a whole lot of trouble. I was a pretty decent student and brought home good grades. I was a frugal, responsible young boy and saved most of the money I made hauling hay and mowing yards. I also sold *Grit* newspapers in our little rural community, which meant that in order to have a paper route with over thirty subscribers, I had to ride my bicycle for about four hours to deliver them once a week. But I did it for the pocket money. *Grit* was a paper laid out a bit like the *National Enquirer,* with colored newsprint pictures, except they wrote about rural farm life, as opposed to salacious celebrity gossip.

After my first job hauling hay, I thought I'd try my hand at sacking groceries at the local Piggly Wiggly. I hated that job because I had to wear a tie, and because the checkout ladies constantly chewed me out if I didn't sack the groceries fast enough and just right. This was before the days of "paper or plastic." Back then you got a big ol' thick paper sack whether you liked it or not. I was expected to stack the groceries inside so that the bag would stand straight up. God forbid you break an egg or smash the bread, and I got so tired of dealing with those checkout ladies. They were brutal, so I used to hide in the back behind the stacks of returned Coke bottles. Eventually I got fired for taking too many long breaks, and my dream of becoming assistant, midnight to 6 A.M., every-other-weekend, part-time manager was shattered at age fifteen.

When I wasn't hauling hay, mowing yards, or going to school I was hunting and fishing—because that was really all there was to do. I spent a lot of time deer, duck, or squirrel hunting, and we generally ate what we killed. However, I don't particularly enjoy eating squirrel. Never did, really. I find it stringier and tougher than chicken. I don't like duck very much, either, but I have some friends who claim to have a great recipe that relies on wrapping said fowl in bacon. It seems like a lot of recipes for inedible foods depend entirely on a pork cocoon. Why not discard the shit filler and just enjoy some hog? Having said all that, however, I really enjoy deer meat (or venison if you're a city slicker). Back then we didn't have any wild turkeys, although I have seen a few out in the woods recently when I've gone back home to visit my parents. (Maybe they chose to relocate from Tennessee due to the terrible turkey overcrowding situation there.)

I grew up in a small home with a pasture full of cows out behind the house. Over the back fence of our property was the Bodcau Wildlife Management Area. So some of the best hunting and fishing in the whole state of Louisiana was within walking distance of our house.

I grew up with lots of guns around the house. I started with pellet and BB guns, until my daddy bought a twenty-gauge shotgun for me when I was twelve. Soon after, I bought myself a .22 rifle with money I made selling *Grit* newspapers. It was a little Winchester .22 automatic that I purchased from Aunt Ruth's store. I still own that rifle, and occasionally I shoot it when I'm out on my farm south of Nashville.

I went to school right there in Sarepta, attending first through twelfth grade on the same campus. We had about 350 kids in the entire school, and when I graduated from Sarepta High School in 1980, we had thirty-two students in our graduating class. It's grown some since then. I think there are about 450 students total in the whole school, which now includes a kindergarten. These days there is talk of consolidating with a couple of other schools from nearby towns where there aren't as many people because the economy and growth in those areas has become a little stagnant. I hope the consolidation doesn't happen, personally.

As a high school freshman I was skinny as a rail but pretty athletic for a six-foot-tall, 150-pound string bean kid. I played every sport we had although I liked some a lot more than I did others. I lived for football. Football was my life from the time I was in the seventh grade until the end of my freshman year of college at Louisiana Tech University. I think I enjoyed it so much because I absolutely loved to hit people. I also appreciated the fact that, to me, football encompassed it all: teamwork, camaraderie, brothers in arms, mano a mano, strategy, sacrifice, glory, heartache, and so on. Football is life, encapsulated.

For the Sarepta Hornets, I played outside linebacker and offensive right tackle. I had to play both sides of the ball with two different mind-sets, and I loved it. I was on the field for almost every minute of the game. They let me rest on kickoffs, which was a shame, because I enjoyed running wide open down the field and picking up a good head of steam before planting somebody into the turf.

We had twenty or so kids on the Sarepta High School varsity football team, but actually only about thirteen of us had any business being on the field. The other kids were freshmen and sophomores, and were there mostly to make it look like we had more of a team than we actually did. I was extremely proud of the fact that we were the smallest school in the state of Louisiana to field a football team yet went to the state playoffs during my sophomore and senior years.

During my senior year, my brother Clay joined the team as a freshman and played quarterback for us. Unlike me, Clay played only on offense since he was too small to play defense at the time. Our whole family was so proud of the fact that Clay made all-district that year as a freshman quarterback on the varsity. He was voted all-district every year of his high school career (both offense and defense most seasons) and went on to play ball at Louisiana Tech, too. Another Bulldog!

There was really something special about being on the gridiron with my younger brother. My favorite play on offense was what is commonly called a sprint-out. I would pull off the line from my tackle position and the guard would cover for me while I rolled out to the right with Clay, who would be sprinting behind me with the ball. My attitude was: "God has yet to create a pass rusher that can sack my quarterback when that quarterback is my little brother." If Clay didn't have a receiver open and it looked like I could create a lane to get him ten or fifteen yards down the field, I'd yell out to him, "Come on!" Then we'd take off together down the sideline for a first down.

I didn't feel any small-town pressure under the Friday night lights. The town was stunned that we even made it to the playoffs. Still, I was heartbroken after we lost the opening round my senior year. Our opponents beat us by only a couple of touchdowns. We gave 'em hell.

The other team had forty kids on their roster, and it got a little demoralizing near the end of the first half after we had turned the ball over on offense. I remember having to switch over to play defense, and watching as the big defensive end I had just been blocking ran off the field. Then, he was replaced by a tight end who was exactly the same size, fresh and ready for battle.

I figure we could have hung in there against any team in the state for at least the first half, but we seldom won after the game became a war of attrition. That's what happens when you play for a small rural school. You can't walk off the field just because you're exhausted and feeling sorry for yourself. You stay in the game and find out what you're made of. All too often, in America today, we as parents become so concerned about pumping up our kids' self-esteem, we forget to teach them the value of staying in a tough game and building self-respect, even when you're outnumbered and outgunned as we were that night.

As much as I loved football, I disliked basketball. But they practically forced me to play on the high school team because I was the tallest kid in school. I was the center, and by the end of the first half, I'd almost always have four fouls. I think I might have finished two full games throughout my entire senior year. Sarepta went 0 and 21 in basketball that season. That's right. We didn't win a single game all year. We went from being one of the best football squads to the worst basketball team in the history of our school.

Sarepta High also had a track team, but no track. We tried to get in shape by running through town and around the pastures. I ran the 330 intermediate hurdles and 110 high hurdles, even though I wasn't any good. We'd go off to a track meet and act like a bunch of yokels just because the other schools actually had a track with lines painted on it. Once again, we sucked, but that was okay. We'd made it to the football playoffs that year, and frankly, that was all that mattered.

I HAD MY FIRST CLOSE CALL with death in March 1979 during my junior year of high school. As I was getting ready to drive to school, there was a thick frost on the windshield of my 1955 Chevy truck. Since the defroster didn't work (I don't think it ever did), I melted a porthole-sized spot in the middle of the windshield with the palm of my hand. I started driving east just as the sun was coming up. As I was steering around a bend, suddenly the bright sunlight hit the windshield and caused a really bad glare. I never even saw the school bus that was stopped in front of me. I went right under the back of that school bus going about fifty miles per hour. I didn't even touch the brakes.

If I hadn't been riding in a sturdy '55 Chevrolet truck, I wouldn't be alive today. That old '55 pickup was built like a Sherman tank, and it looked like the impact of the collision just scraped the body of the truck clear off the frame. I went far enough underneath the back of the bus that there were black marks on the bumper of the truck where I hit the back wheels. Thank God, none of the kids on the bus were injured. They even got to stay home from school that day! You're welcome, kiddos.

I, however, was mangled up pretty bad. My knees were cut up and I broke a couple of ribs that punctured my right lung. The hood came through the windshield, cut up my eye, folded back the skin on my fingers, and severed my nose. My great uncle, Aunt Ruth's husband, lived just down the road from where it happened. He and a friend actually heard the accident all the way from their house. They hurried down and saw that it was me. Since they thought there was not enough time to wait for an ambulance, Uncle Cecil and his buddy propped me up in the middle of the bench seat of his pickup truck and sped off north toward Springhill. I remember looking in the rearview mirror and seeing my face. It looked like a slab of bloody meat hanging down off my skull. My nose was dangling by a single piece of skin. I guess I was in shock and out of my head.

"Hey! Uncle Cecil! Look!" I said, pulling my nose up and down off my face.

"Stop doing that, son!" he said, with a nauseated look on his face.

We got to the Springhill Hospital emergency room and I don't remember too much else. They had two doctors on duty in the emergency room that morning. Both were fine country doctors that I had known all my life, friends to myself and my family. That has to be a strange situation for a physician to find himself in.

When I finally came to, I was laid up in my hospital room. A state trooper came in and presented me with a ticket for failure to maintain control. Now . . . if I had tried to stop and couldn't, that would have been a failure to maintain control. However, since I at no time . . . Oh, forget it. Thanks, gooberhead!

I'd been awake most of the day when the nurse told me I needed some rest. Mama was about to leave, but I asked her to stay.

"Don't go, Mama. I'm not going to sleep."

"Why?"

There was no doubt in my mind. I was shaken up pretty badly and I felt death looming over me, but I figured that as long as I stayed awake I could fight off the Grim Reaper. If I dozed off to sleep it would be like I was giving up, and I wasn't going to do that. Eventually they gave me something to calm me down because I was too freaked out to close my eyes. It's a scary thing to deal with when you're seventeen and you wake up strapped to all these machines and tubes. My whole head was wrapped up in layers and layers of gauze and bandages. I looked like a mummy. The only thing visible on my face was one eye and an opening for my mouth. I had tubes stuck in and out of me, with blood running out of one tube coming out of my lung. After several weeks, I finally healed up, and for years after, whenever Dr. Sessions, one of the physicians on duty, would run into me on the street, he'd always say, "Come over here boy and let's have a look at that nose." And then he'd show anyone else who might be around, "See? No plastic surgery! I put that nose back on myself!" Today there's only a tiny scar on the left side of my nose that's barely noticeable. Atta boy, Doc!

That was the first time I had cheated death, and there would be plenty more close calls. In 2006, I cut a song called "I Came Here to Live," which captured the spirit of my childhood in Sarepta.

"I came here to live," the song says. "I didn't come here to die."

The morning I killed my precious truck, I had chosen life. Later on, making that choice to survive would get a whole lot tougher.

Chapter Four

UNIONS: GOOD, BAD, OR OUTMODED?

TODAY, ONLY 7 PERCENT OF AMERICAN WORKERS BELONG to a trade union. When unions were created back in the day, they were absolutely necessary. Workers were being abused and mistreated, there were no child labor laws, work environments were unsafe—the list goes on and on. It was terrible. Now we have OSHA, and lots of state and federal regulations, and the old kind of working atmosphere simply cannot exist. Nowadays workers in this country are protected against seedy work conditions. They may need union protections in other countries, but I just don't see it so much in this country. I really don't.

There could be an argument about whether or not wages are high enough. That's fine. We can discuss that. But as far as ensuring that there are civilized working conditions, do we still need unions?

Take my hometown of Sarepta, Louisiana, in the northwest corner of the state. When I was growing up, most of the working men in Sarepta and Springhill were employed at a huge paper mill owned by International Paper Company. International Paper also had a corrugating plant there, but the paper mill was the really big operation. Both towns survived because of that mill. In 1979, as I was going into my senior year in high school, the union contract came up for renegotiation.

The union had gotten things to the point where there were so many shop rules, if one guy needed help moving something, the guy right next to him wasn't allowed to pitch in. The waggle worker couldn't assist the widget worker or the union would file a grievance. All the waggle worker could do was stand there and say, "I see you're about to break your freaking back trying to lift that widget. And you could possibly fall and kill yourself, 'cause that's too heavy for you. But I can't help you, 'cause the union says I can't. It's not my gig."

Naturally the company wanted some flexibility on the work rules, but the union wouldn't budge. In fact, the union representatives went in with *even more* demands. So International Paper said, "Look, the guys running your union must not be reading the financial pages. We can't make this paper mill pay on your terms, so everybody can go home. We're selling the mill to a company in Germany. You're all out of a job."

That's what the union did to its own members. The German company didn't choose to operate the paper mill; its deal with International Paper was high finance, an asset swap to move their tax liabilities around. Only now, twenty five years later, is Sarepta beginning to recover. At one time you could buy a nice brick house in town just by taking up the note on it at the bank.

One of my uncles and a lot of other people we knew who worked in that paper mill lost their jobs. Luckily, my father worked in the corrugating plant, which International Paper kept operating with paper that they trucked in from another mill. My father narrowly avoided a family crisis and he knew it. That experience put a bad taste in my mouth for unions, and nothing since has made it taste any better.

Look at the car companies. Sure, the executives at Ford, GM, and Chrysler bear plenty of blame for not keeping up with the foreign car makers and not making more fuel-efficient models, but a huge part of the problem is the United Auto Workers having a stranglehold on their plants.

General Motors recently dropped behind Toyota for total car sales in the United States. Toyota knocks GM out of the top spot in GM's own backyard. In my opinion, there's one reason for that and it's not the quality of the product that General Motors puts out. It's just three letters: *UAW*.

That's partly why Ford is in such bad financial shape and lost $12.7 billion in 2006. And it's also why Chrysler is eliminating eleven thousand blue-collar jobs and two thousand white collar positions in 2007 and 2008 to try to stay competitive. GM has had its problems, too, and it's partly because they've got guys working in those plants making damn good money standing on an assembly line. They stick this part in that car when it comes by and they're making top dollar plus all these expensive health and pension benefits. It's harder to justify that in today's world market. No wonder these plants are moving across the border to Mexico.

Today Toyota, Honda, Nissan, Mercedes-Benz, and BMW are all making cars profitably in this country, and paying good wages, too, but they're not locked into a dance of death with the UAW. American automakers are at a major disadvantage because for every car that rolls off a Michigan assembly line, far too much profit is being siphoned off to pay for expensive benefit packages and pension schemes for retired workers and executives. These are operating costs that the Japanese and German factories in the United States aren't saddled with. Then, adding insult to injury, our government lets Japan charge a value-added tax to all the cars we export into their country! You'd think our politicians would use our large American retail market as a better bargaining chip. When are the free trade advocates in this country going to loosen up a little and admit that our foreign trading partners are cheating us under the table in this card game, and that we all need to play by the same set of rules?

While I don't disagree that Japanese cars may be better, I'm still not going to drive one. I've always owned GM products and that's all I intend to own. I guess I'm a hopeless romantic. I keep hoping that GM will turn around someday soon and that the ship will right itself.

I HAD A UNION HASSLE of my own when I first came to Nashville and got a record deal. The label called me up after the recording contract went through.

"Trace, you gotta go down and join the union."

"I don't want to join the union," I told them.

"Well you have to. If you go on television or something, that's how you're going to get paid. The union is going to collect your money for you and your check is going to come to you through the union."

"But I don't want to be in the union," I insisted, stubborn as a mule.

"Well you have to."

We left it at that, but I was determined not to have anything to do with them. Finally I went down and had one initial meeting with the guy at the union hall. It was uneventful. I walked into his office and sat there for ten minutes and listened to his little spiel. I barely paid any attention to what the guy had to say. Then I said, "Have a good day," and I walked out.

I haven't been back, and I've never again spoken to anybody from their office. Then after I had been in the union for several months, my business manager got a phone call from the union of-

fice and they told him, "Look, we've been sending all of our corre-
spondence to Trace Adkins and we're not hearing anything back
from him. His dues aren't paid."

My business manager called me and asked me what the hell
was going on.

"Yeah I've been getting that shit from them, but I don't even
open it. I just throw that stuff in the trash. I suggest they send the
important material to you because I'm still not gonna open any
letters from the union. I'll just throw the envelope in the garbage.
Hell, I don't even care if there's a check in it."

That reminds me (for some unexplained reason) of something
else . . .

Folks ask me how I feel about Wal-Mart being so grotesquely
big and powerful in this country. Are superstores like Wal-Mart
good or bad for the average American small town and its working
men and women? Right now they're the people's choice.

You know what? That's a double-edged-sword question. I almost don't know how I really feel about that, to tell you the truth.
I can see both sides of the issue. Sure, I feel bad for mom-and-pop
businesses when Wal-Mart comes in and shuts them down, but
God, don't you just love going to Wal-Mart? Everything you need
is in one big place! You don't have to go anywhere else. There's a
nice rickety old man who smiles through yellow dentures, says
hello when you walk in the door, and shoves a basket at you. I
mean, you can have your tires rotated, buy some groceries, get your
hemorrhoid cream, pick up some golf balls, and fill a prescription
all under one roof. Plus they sell more of my records, hands down,
than anybody—probably more than all the other CD retail outlets
put together. So I have to say, "More power to 'em."

I've also been told a few times by music business gatekeepers,
"Man, I don't know if we can put that sexy song on your record.

Wal-Mart might not sell the album with it on there." Well, I've been warned about that before, but nothing has ever happened so I don't worry about it too much. I don't have a problem with Wal-Mart. Other people might, but I really don't. In addition to jobs, poor folks get more bang for their buck when they shop at Wal-Mart, while the rich folks look down their noses. The last time I checked, in America, if people in a community don't want something like a superstore built in their backyard, they're free to organize and let their voices be heard.

Chapter Five

DADDY SANG BASS

OUNTRY MUSIC HAS A WHOLE BUNCH OF ALL-AMERICAN influences—gospel, blues, bluegrass, Western music, Western swing, Cajun, rockabilly, folk, Southern rock, or more specifically, Haggard, Hank, and the Grand Ole Opry. But as for my thing, it all started with Southern gospel or so-called country gospel. Country gospel first became popular in the early 1900s, and is most readily associated with what we call "quartet music," that is, the four-male vocal combo of tenor, lead, baritone, and bass voices. Since I'm a bass singer myself, if it hadn't been for my early interest in Southern gospel, I would never have had a career in music.

Performing in front of strangers wasn't something that came naturally to me. It became a job I worked my way into because I was a shy kid. In fact, I'm still kind of brooding and shy. I may have a reputation in Nashville for being a Louisiana redneck, but not for being a showboat. I'm just not an outgoing type of person. I can't walk into a room, meet and greet everybody, and do the networking dance. I'm sometimes withdrawn and almost timid. I am not comfortable "working" the room, and I don't automatically open up to people at first. Sometimes my standoffishness gets misconstrued as being uppity. If I don't know you, I'm going to be kind of bashful.

Though I dreamed of becoming a country music singer as a teenager, I never imagined I'd actually become a stage performer. By the time I hit high school, I was already messing around with the guitar. A friend of mine, Jeff, who played bass, and another pal, Danny, who was a good singer and a pretty decent drummer, and myself had been goofing around together to the point where we thought we had something going that resembled a band. If any one of our homes would have had a garage, we would have been a "garage" band. We were a "tool shed" band instead.

Right around that time, my church was set on having a banquet. There was a trio of guys scheduled to sing at this banquet. Somebody suggested that my friends and I play behind this gospel-singing trio and I thought, okay, that might be fun. We rehearsed at the church, worked hard, and learned the material these three gentlemen would be singing. During rehearsals, I stood in the back with my guitar. I had learned all the songs, knew the words, and began hearing a bass vocal line rumbling in my head. So I started singing my own bass part way back from where the gospel trio stood with their mics. The lead singer heard me singing, stopped the song, then turned around and asked me, "Is that you?"

"Yeah," I mumbled apologetically. "Sorry."

"No, wait a minute," he said. "Do you know the song well enough that you can sing the bass part?"

"Yeah, I reckon I can manage it if you want me to."

"C'mon up here, son, and do it."

And that's how it happened. I joined up with the trio and started singing bass at age seventeen. The little banquet gig we did went over so well, they invited us to sing the same songs at the very next Sunday service. So we got up there and did our gospel quartet act. After that I sang more and more in church almost every other week or so. Pretty soon the word spread among the other congregations in the area, and they invited us to come to their little churches and do our gospel quartet thing. I was no front man at the time. I could only perform as a part of a group. Outside of silly school plays, that was my first experience being onstage.

By then I had become a big fan of bass singers like Richard Sterban of the Oak Ridge Boys and Harold Reid of the Statler Brothers. I found I really enjoyed the performing part of quartet music, and got into the theatrics of doing the whole bass singer thing, where you drop to one knee, and watch the young church girls giggle and elbow each other. Chicks dig the bass singer. They love it when you hit that ultralow note and it kind of rumbles and they get tickled.

Within a couple of years, we had sung in practically every Protestant church within a hundred miles of Sarepta. The biggest gig we ever did was on the lawn of the state capitol in Baton Rouge in front of Governor David Treen. We were among twenty-five other quartets there that day, including the Masters V featuring J. D. Sumner, arguably the best bass singer in history. As I stood on the side of the stage and listened to him, I realized that I sang bass like a twelve-year-old girl. Relatively speaking.

We called ourselves the New Commitments. We sang with only a piano and a bass guitar. No drums. We played mainstream Christian country gospel, not unlike the Hinsons and Bill Gaither, but mostly we covered songs (as best we could) by other quartets like the Cathedrals, the Inspirations, and the Florida Boys. We even released a couple of homegrown LPs that we produced ourselves.

For me, the gospel experience was more musical than evangelical, but there were times when things would get spiritually wild and crazy. Once, I got a jolt of the Holy Ghost when I began sitting in with this Pentecostal group. I was about nineteen when a guy who lived nearby in Springhill called me. He had a Pentecostal group going and he wanted me to come and sing with them for a couple of shows. It was him and a couple of ladies. While he sang lead, the ladies sang the alto and tenor parts, and I sang bass and played guitar. It was the first time I'd ever sung with girls. It was a cool mix of voices, one I'd never experienced before, and I dug it immediately.

The music this Pentecostal group performed was a lot more like traditional country music than what the New Commitments played. It was essentially country music with gospel lyrics, and man, we did some rockin' stuff and a lot of up-tempo material. Basically, we were a Hinson cover band.

I remember playing an Apostolic church one night in Arkansas when, all of a sudden, the people began screaming and hollering and then started running laps around the inside of the church! The vibe was infectious. A rush of pure adrenaline washed through me. I suddenly felt hot all over my body. I got fired up and hit my guitar so hard I busted three strings. I don't mean to be sacrilegious here, but when people say they're overcome with the Holy Ghost, I often wonder if perhaps they're feeling that same adrenaline rush I felt that night. Just wondering.

I eventually left the whole gospel music scene behind. It started one night when I was about to sing at this Pentecostal church and the pastor came out to the bus right before the show. He looked right at me and said, "I'm sorry, son, but I'm afraid I can't let you sing in my church."

"Why not?"

"Your hair's too long. I can't let you in looking like that."

"I don't know what his deal is," I told the bandleader that

night, "but there's nothing wrong with me. If I'm not good enough to sing in his church, I can't be a part of this anymore. I'm done."

And that marked the end of my gospel singing career.

Playing gospel music was an extremely rewarding and valuable experience. That's where I first got the bug, the itch, to perform live, and it also helped me to gain confidence. After singing at church, I would take my guitar out on Saturday nights to do a guest song at shows like the North Louisiana Hayride or the Columbia County Jamboree. It gave me the opportunity to play in front of a dance hall audience, backed by a pretty good house band. I suppose it was like early karaoke, except with a live band. I'd slip in an hour or so before the show, tell the band which song I was going to sing and in which key. Usually the musicians already knew the tune. Then it was time to step up to the mic and do it. I'm sure I sucked at first, but at least I was out in front of a live crowd getting my feet wet singing country music.

Chapter Six

AMERICAN STARS AND BARS

ONCE DID SOME RESEARCH ON MY FAMILY TREE ON MY daddy's side, but I wasn't too proud of what I discovered. Here's what happened to my ancestor on my dad's side, four grandfathers ago. For our purposes, we'll just call him Grandpa Adkins. During the War for Southern Independence, if you had a thousand dollars, you could pay for somebody to go in your place. That's exactly what he did. He gave the government one thousand dollars and sent his brother in his stead. So, his brother went off to war and because his mother was elderly and fragile, he stayed behind and ran the plantation. Grandpa Adkins thought, and for good reason, that his dear brother would get killed and never come back. So he had his mother sign over all the property to him and put everything in his name.

Well, his brother lived through the war and came back, and they fought over the farm in the court system for years and years. I was brokenhearted to read about it. I expected my forefather to be some colorful, pistol-wielding Confederate Civil War hero, but he took a different path. I chose not to even remember his name.

My grandmother's maiden name on my dad's side was Giles, and I know that her family came to Louisiana from Tennessee. It seems ironic that I've gone full circle by moving my family to Tennessee.

There were also Adkinses who came from Tennessee. They were from the eastern part of the state, specifically Teleco Plains near Cleveland, Tennessee. So there's a lot of Tennessee ancestry in my blood from my father's side of the family.

MY FASCINATION WITH the war began as a kid when my grand-daddy on my mother's side, J. T. Carraway, told me about his granddaddy. I feel as if this generation of kids won't have the same close association with history as I did. I only had to go back two "greats" on my mother's side to get to the Civil War. My grand-daddy's granddaddy, Henry T. Morgan, served in the 31st Louisiana Infantry. He was wounded, taken prisoner, and then paroled in Vicksburg. He had to sign a document promising that he would never again take up arms against the federal government. Then he reenlisted in the Confederate Army about three months later, although I don't think he was in a major engagement after that.

I've been a Civil War enthusiast all my life. When I visited the battlefield in Vicksburg and stood in a trench (the actual trenches are still there) where my great-great-granddaddy stood, I felt as if I had been there before. Kind of the way, I suppose, General George Patton felt when he visited the ancient battlefields in Europe. Tears came to my eyes. It moved me tremendously.

Sometimes I think I'm a man born in the wrong century. For example, I recently went under the knife for some minor surgery. And while I don't remember saying this (I was just coming around in the recovery room), when the doctor asked me what kind of pain medication I preferred, I asked for laudanum. Laudanum was an opium-based liquid painkiller that they largely depended on in the nineteenth century. It was sweetened with sugar and was sometimes referred to as the "wine of opium." That's what I asked for. How goofy is that?

I can recall sitting and talking to my granddaddy, and asking him what he knew about the Civil War. That's when it hit me. When he was my age, he could sit and talk with *his* granddaddy who had actually been there!

For me, there are two pivotal points in American history. One is the American Revolution, which founded the beloved country we have today, and the second is the American Civil War: the War Between the States, or the Second American Revolution, as I've heard it called. Whatever name you choose to use. I like all the old-school terms. The War Against Northern Aggression. The War for Southern Independence—which is really what it was.

The true definition of a civil war is war between factions, re-gions, or citizens of the same country. A popular misconception is that the South was out to overthrow the government. Nobody in the South was out to overthrow the republic. It's just that the South no longer wanted to be subservient to the United States government. You can argue whether or not the Confederate states had the constitutional right to secede—and of course states no longer have that right—but at the time, the South argued the point that they did have the right to leave. The South never in-vaded the North in order to take over the government. They wanted to part ways and do their own thing. Yet, technically, in a sense, they did overthrow the state governments once the Confed-eracy was set up.

There are plenty of misconceptions about the war, and espe-cially in the way it's taught today in public schools. Like most wars, the Civil War was fought over money, yet revisionists today have made it almost 100 percent about slavery. I have my own ideas and conclusions based on a lot of reading and study. While the North had become industrialized, the South remained an agrarian society. While the North was *importing* industrial goods from Europe, the South was *exporting* agricultural commodities like cotton and tobacco to Europe. As the products from the South were flowing one way toward Europe, the money was flowing the opposite way, directly into the South's coffers. Since the North wasn't exporting much, and they were importing everything from Europe in order to construct their industrial empire, tensions grew over the number one cause of war. M-o-n-e-y. The South was all about exporting goods and making lots of money. The North was about financing industry.

Yes, it's true, the South made money in an immoral way, on the backs of slaves. But at the time, slavery was a dying institution and it didn't require a war to bring about what was already inevitable. Slavery certainly made no sense morally and soon it would make no sense financially. It was on the verge of becoming economically defunct with the invention of Eli Whitney's cotton gin. Here was a machine that you didn't have to feed, clothe, or house—all you needed were mules to pull it.

While the Civil War was brutal on both sides, the South has always gotten an unfair shake and a bad rep because of the way revisionists have tried to make isolated incidences of barbarism the rule rather than the exception. But in reality, the brutality of America's bloodiest war swung both ways. The Jayhawkers in Kansas were ruthless murderers. If a family had Southern sympathies or relatives, they were often slaughtered and their houses burned to the ground. End of story. That's the reason I've always hated the fact that athletes from the University of Kansas can be called Jayhawks, yet people get pissed off because the University of Mississippi athletes call themselves the Ole Miss Rebels. It's not right that the Jayhawks can represent a murderous group of vigilantes who killed people indiscriminately while people look down their noses at a symbol of Southern pride.

Bill Maher once asked me why, when I talk about this stuff, he senses a fire still burning inside me. That's because Southerners can look back on their history and see an invading, conquering army coming in and burning down their hometowns. Northerners have no such reference in their history. They also didn't have a William Tecumseh Sherman waging war on the civilian population. Okay, you can hate him for what he did to cities like Atlanta, but man, at least the guy was a forward thinker. He knew where modern warfare was headed when he staged his infamous march through the South. His plan was to wage war on the civilian population so that once it got painful enough for the people, the outcry for peace would become so loud, the Confederate military leaders would have no choice but to surrender. Sherman's plan was to end the war by making war. He marched through Georgia and South Carolina burning everything in his path, just as Union General Philip Sheridan did in 1864 when he destroyed the Shenandoah Valley. Sheridan had similar orders from his superiors in Washington, D.C., who told him they didn't "want a crow flying over the Shenandoah Valley to be able to come down and find anything to eat."

That's total war and that's the way wars should be fought. Unfortunately, it's no longer the way we do it. That's the problem our military has in Iraq. We don't go to war to end the war. War is the last resort and if you try to pretty it up for the politicians, the voters, and the press, it's never going to be effective.

I'm deeply proud to be a descendent of the Confederacy, which is not always a cool thing to say. Everybody's always stirred up about the Confederate flag, mainly because supremacist groups, like the Ku Klux Klan, took it and soiled it and transformed it into something dirty. There were so many gallant, courageous men who fought under that banner and it's sad that people now equate it with racism, because that's not what it stood for. People are generally misinformed. The Confederate flag as most people know it was a battle flag, and that's all it was—carried in battle basically to keep the ranks in proper marching order. The Stars and Bars, the Confederacy's national flag, was a different flag. A red, white, and blue striped flag with a little blue field up in the corner with thirteen stars in a circle, or eleven depending on who made the flag. (There was always a discrepancy whether there were eleven or thirteen states in the Confederacy. I myself say there were twelve. Kentucky doesn't count. They never seemed to get with the program. But I count Missouri because there was a lot of bloodletting *in* Missouri and a lot of men who fought for the Confederacy were *from* Missouri.)

Most of my inspirational historical heroes are Civil War figures. I dig George Patton and Douglas MacArthur, men who knew how to fight, but Nathan Bedford Forrest has always been my favorite character in military history. As a young man, he rose through the ranks despite having very little formal education. He moved to Memphis, and became a slave broker, a plantation owner, and a wealthy man. However, when Tennessee left the Union and joined the Confederacy in 1861, he put together a company of men (cavalry actually) and paid for their provisions with his own money. He entered the Confederate Army as a private and ended up a major general. His men would obey him or else. He killed a couple of his own soldiers and threatened his superiors on several occasions. He was a badass before anybody knew what that term meant. It was Nathan Bedford Forrest who said about war, "War to the knife. Knife to the hilt."

That is, when you run out of bullets you go to the knife, and you bury the knife to the hilt. That's how you should fight, period.

The reason nobody has ever made a movie of Forrest's life (outside of Forrest Gump being named after him) was the Fort Pillow incident, where he gave no quarter. The deal he made with Union soldiers was to surrender or be killed. Fort Pillow was being manned by black troops from the South who had signed on to fight with the North, so when Forrest's boys went in there, they started killing everyone. Forrest has always been blamed for that incident, yet it wasn't entirely his fault. While he didn't do enough to stop it, he never actually issued the order for all those men to be killed. Still, that incident has badly marred his legacy.

Then again, Forrest did join the Ku Klux Klan when the Klan first started out as a good ol' boy fraternity formed to protect white Southerners' rights. This was in the Reconstruction era when the carpetbaggers and the Union interlopers were put in charge of Southern state governments. Ultimately, however, the Klan evolved into an ugly night rider organization, and that's when Forrest officially disbanded the early version of the Klan. He didn't approve of what the Klan was doing and by the end of his life was virtually making civil rights speeches for racial equality. Forrest was truly an enigma well worth studying.

It's no mystery to me why Southern people are still passionate about the War Between the States, more so than most other people in this country and much more so than Northerners and Westerners. My home state, Louisiana, was one of the last states (the others were Florida and South Carolina) to remain under martial law with a military governor, actually, until 1877, twelve long years after the official surrender of the Confederacy. Therefore, because of Northern corruption and the carpetbagger taxes that were levied, many families lost everything they had, including property that had been in Louisiana families for generations.

I understand the moral arguments about how Louisianans probably wouldn't have held that much property if it hadn't been for slavery. I guess my family's ancestors lost their property, too, because I certainly don't have any of it. So the effects of the Civil War are still felt 150 years later.

I'm a lifetime member of the Sons of Confederate Veterans. It's an organization for people who wish to preserve and respect the heritage and history of the War Against Northern Aggression. It sometimes gets a bad rap in the press when narrow-minders (I just made that word up, I think) claim that it's simply a racist organization. I'm not saying that there aren't some racists in it. There probably are. But I think the large majority of members are people who don't want history to forget the brave and gallant men who fought for the Confederacy. They're our ancestors. Yet we as Americans have tried to erase them from our history books, citing the Civil War as an ugly chapter in American history. So some say let's just forget about the whole thing.

I realize that to the victor go the spoils, so the victor gets to write history however he chooses. And while we did have abolitionists in the North who were passionate about abolishing slavery, it should also be noted that it was a minority of people in the South who actually owned slaves. When my great-great-grandfather, Henry T. Morgan, whose daughter was my granddaddy's mother, was a private in the 31st Louisiana Infantry, he was a poor hog farmer from Claiborne Parish, Louisiana. He didn't own any cotton fields. He went to war because Union troops invaded his homeland. He didn't fight for the Confederacy to keep his slaves. He didn't have any. Not one.

So, I say no! Let's not forget the Civil War. Let's revere those men for who they were, heroes on both sides who fought in the bloodiest war in this nation's history. And "no" is why a lot of Southern men went to war. Rather than having a government's will forced upon them, they picked up a rifle and said no. So yes, I am a proud member of the Sons of Confederate Veterans.

I guess I am what people call a history buff. I believe in avoiding future mistakes by studying history and the mistakes of the past. The one person I regret never meeting was historian and author Shelby Foote. The first book I read by him was about the siege of Vicksburg, where, as I said, my great-great-granddaddy was taken prisoner. After reading that book, I immediately became a Shelby Foote fan. I went so far as contacting someone who knew him. I knew he didn't sign his books because such an act of vanity offended him. Apparently he was somewhat reclusive and didn't much like the fanfare that went along with being a famous author. Foote was more of a historian and a scholar. As I found out, when you went to meet him, you arrived bearing a gift. He especially liked to smoke a pipe. So the guy I contacted gave me the name of a smoke shop in Memphis where Shelby Foote bought his pipes. Unfortunately, I never followed up and met Foote, mainly because I was so in awe of the man. I was a little shy and intimidated to make his acquaintance. He died in 2005.

We Southerners are the only folks whose ancestors know what it feels like to lose a war fought on American soil. While the South could never have won the war militarily, what they were trying to do was drag it out long enough so that the peaceniks in the North would eventually scream for peace. I guess the Confederacy knew long before anyone else did how to defeat the United States military. Their tactic was to make the campaign as miserable and as lengthy as they could (what we today call "being bogged down") so that eventually the Yankees would just go away. It didn't work that way, because of Abraham Lincoln's resolve.

The Civil War was essentially fought over states' rights, a concept that gets glossed over as if "states' rights" was a slogan that somebody pulled out of thin air and didn't have any real meaning. But it did have meaning. It still has meaning. States are still saying to the federal government, "You are not going to dictate to us how we may conduct our lives in our own state."

Today, instead of the blue and the gray, we now have blue states and red states. As we the people of the United States of America become more fragmented and less united, I believe we'll see more and more states going their own way, passing their own laws, to the point where people will have to choose which state to live in based on which key laws each state passes in its own legislature. It's not just a conservative or liberal matter, it's more of a lifestyle choice. For instance, if you believe in abortion rights, you need to live in New York. If you oppose abortion, live in Alabama or South Dakota. If you believe in gay marriage, you might want to move to Massachusetts. If you're against motorcycle helmet laws, then you can reside in Arizona. Strict or less strict gun laws. Medical marijuana. These are but a few state issues that now dictate where people can ideologically choose to live in the United States. And maybe that's not such a bad thing, as long as Americans are free to travel and live in whatever state best fits their lifestyle and beliefs. That's what states' rights means to me today.

Chapter Seven

ROUGHNECKIN' OFFSHORE

EVERYONE HAS CONFIDENCE BUILDERS IN THEIR LIVES. Singing in a gospel quartet helped me conquer stage fright. Playing football also gave me confidence. When I entered my freshman year of college in 1980, I was in the best shape of my life, ready to play football. Although I had plans to become a petroleum engineer, I entered Louisiana Tech primarily to play ball. Unfortunately, my knees didn't make the grade. By the spring of my freshman year, I had dislocated my kneecap twice.

The doctor didn't beat around the bush. "Son," he told me, "I can put this knee together, but if you have thoughts of playing more college ball or turning pro, forget about it. It's not going to happen. Your knee is simply not going to hold together. One more injury and I might not be able to put you back together without a limp." I knew it was time for me to hang up my cleats. Football was over for me. It has now become a spectator sport to be viewed religiously at every opportunity.

After attending public school in a small, rural community, college was a huge shock for me. I didn't have the tools to deal with it. When my football days were over, I struggled through another year before I chose to drop out. I wasn't equipped to deal with the intense study regimen at Louisiana Tech. I didn't know how to study because I went to a public school where everything was graded on a curve so that all thirty-two kids in my senior class could graduate. I didn't have to study much to graduate third in my class, so high school didn't prepare me for college.

In Sarepta, I knew where every one of my thirty-one class-mates lived; I knew where they went to church; I knew where their parents worked. I'd known them all my life. We grew up together. If you graduate with a class of thirty-one "family members" and go on to a major engineering school with twenty thousand students, you're completely freaked out, at first.

Looking back, I wish that I had had somebody leaning on me harder to make sure I stayed in school, but that didn't happen. My old man always gave me just enough leeway to let me have my own experiences and learn from my own mistakes.

After my sophomore year in college, I was still in love with my high school sweetheart, Barbara Lewis. So I toyed with the idea of getting a job, and getting married. Since my father had been work-ing for the paper company in the corrugating division, I asked him if he could help me get a job out at the plant. He surprised me with his reply.

"Yeah, I could get you a job out there, but I'm not going to."

"Why not? I need a job. Why won't you help me?"

"You'd only get stuck out there like I did. If you go to work in a factory, you'll get vested in the retirement plan and the health in-surance, and you'll end up thinking you can never leave. If you want to go up there and fill out an application, go right ahead, I'm not going to stop you, but I'm not going to put a word in for you."

I didn't even bother to fill out an application. I didn't want to work where my old man worked, and know that each and every day he didn't want me there.

Looking back at what my father did, I realize that he was kicking me out of the nest. Maybe he thought I had potential to go on and do something different or maybe he was punishing me for quitting school. When he graduated from Sarepta High in 1960, he was all-state in football. A real hoss. He could have gone on to play college ball, but he didn't. Instead, he stayed behind, got married, and then I came along.

At the end of the 1981-82 school year I was not sure if I wanted to continue in the field of petroleum technology. That summer, I found a job working in the oil field so I decided to take a break from college and started working in the petroleum industry full time. I never went back to school. I was already making good money and I was developing confidence in myself as a good "hand." At the time I was laying pipelines, hooking up tank batteries, and setting up pumping units. Oil field production grunt work.

At first I resented the fact that my old man wouldn't help me get a job at his plant, but that resentment didn't last very long. Once I started learning the ropes in the oil field and saw how exciting and dangerous that job could be, I felt like I was in the right place. It was tough work, but it was fun. Once the well was properly drilled, my job was to help hook up the lines so that the oil could be pumped into tanks and transported to refineries. We laid a lot of pipelines. I was young and in good shape. It was hard, strenuous work, but I found it satisfying.

I saw guys getting mangled and hurt on the job, and it happened to me a couple of times. The first time I got injured was when I was working as a swamper for a truck driver going out to oil fields and picking up tanks. We were picking up a mud mixer at one location, and as we were pulling it up onto the back of a flatbed truck, it got hung up. I saw the thirty-foot steel tank shift. Right about that time, a cable snapped and hit me right across the forehead and busted my head open. Had I not ducked, it could have been a whole lot worse. It might have cut my throat. But I ducked just in time, so it only caught my forehead. I damn near got killed, and for the second time I had escaped death.

Blood was running down my face. I played it down, but one of the tool pushers on the location decided to take me to the hospital in his truck. On the ride over, the old boy gave me some hard-earned advice. "Son, you're not going to work in the oil field for longer than five years without getting hurt bad enough to miss work." He told me his hips were made of plastic because he had been crushed by some drill pipe.

Not long after, I was working with two very close friends of mine, Devin and David. We were standing next to a four-hundred-barrel tank made of fiberglass. It had a leak that we were repairing when suddenly there was a loud boom. The tank exploded with four hundred barrels of brine in it. I remember coming to after being washed several yards away from the tank. As I got up on my knees I could see David, already on his feet and calling for Devin. I got up and called out, and then I spotted him.

Over toward the tank, or what was left of it, was a huge piece of fiberglass, and I could see Devin underneath it. I grabbed the fiberglass, flipped it off him, and scooped him up in my arms. Acting on adrenaline—I had no idea where I was going—I ran toward the field office. Devin was obviously badly injured, swallowing his tongue and convulsing. As we waited for the ambulance, I felt horrible. I loved this guy, and I was the one who had gotten him the job. We used to haul hay together as kids during the summers and played high school sports together the rest of the year. Devin was my hunting and fishing buddy. Now, my best friend was unconscious in my arms.

I didn't even realize that my leg had been mashed in the accident. It was bruised so deeply that I had to have therapy for the next couple of weeks to break up the blood clots. I didn't break any bones, but my leg was black as night. It was another close call but I knew I'd be all right. Devin stayed in a coma for almost a month, but he survived.

I was around twenty when I first went to work in the oil field. I waited until I was twenty-three before I bought a house and got married. We moved into a fourteen-by-sixty-foot trailer house, which I bought for sixteen thousand dollars. Barbara and I lived in that trailer for the next five or six years, and I loved it. The coolest thing about trailers is that if things get too bad where you are, you can just hook up to it with your monster truck and get the hell out. They do, however, depreciate a little. I eventually sold it for five thousand dollars.

Pretty soon I made the big move from land-based oil field production to offshore drilling work on a rig in the Gulf of Mexico. When I got the job offshore, I had my own routine going—two weeks on, two weeks off. I worked hard, ate well, and by the end of those two working weeks, I was clean, healthy, strong, and ready to rock. Once I got home, I'd party for a few days and get things done around the trailer. Once I got close to going back offshore, I'd get a little depressed . . . so I'd drink a little bit during the last few off days. After a couple of days back offshore the alcohol would be out of my system, followed by another ten or eleven days of good clean living, hard work, and, of course, good food. Plus there were drug tests to consider, and I wasn't stupid enough to be caught doing drugs, or anything else that might show up in my piss. That was probably another reason I drank alcohol. The harmless drug.

One night I was driving in my truck to Jackson, Mississippi, to ride with my driller (my boss) to go back offshore. I drove through a tornado in Vicksburg, and I didn't even realize I'd done it. I only found out after the fact. It was raining hard. It was a bad storm. All of a sudden, my truck started hydroplaning and spinning out of control. I ended up stuck in a ditch waiting for a tow truck to come pull me out. The running boards were torn off my truck. Again.

I was having a smoke and kicking myself in the balls for driving too fast in that kind of weather when a state trooper showed up and he asked me, "Did y'all see that tornado?"

"What tornado?"

"The one that just came through here."

"Oh, the one that blew me into the f**king ditch?"

I didn't feel quite so bad.

After about three years on the rig, I was as good a derrick hand as there was in the Gulf of Mexico. I was the cock of the walk when I walked onto that rig with a "don't f**k with me" oil field trash swagger. I *knew* there wasn't a better hand in the Gulf than me. Nobody could roughneck better than I could.

I'd fly out to the rig and stay my two weeks. At first I started out roustabouting. Unloading boats. Scrubbing decks. Painting. Whatever needed doing. I did that for about six months, but I wanted to be on the drill floor with the drill crew because that's where the real action happened. I got the promotion and knew I was where I wanted to be. Roughnecking.

Roughnecking is when you're part of the drill crew on the rig floor making connections and tripping pipe. Your mission statement is to keep it on the bottom, turning to the right. Makin' hole!

Suddenly I had a career future with options. I could either go on to the drill crew or I could remain a roustabout in hopes of one day becoming a crane operator. Or I could possibly go on to the engineering department and become a motorman. But I knew I wanted to be on the drill crew because that's where the cowboys were. It was assholes and elbows all the time. High intensity.

Loyal teamwork. Fast connections and hard honest work. Today it's so automated that roughnecks don't even have to make connections anymore. Everything's done by robots. But I was at the tail end of the old school days when roughnecking was still roughnecking.

I eventually worked my way up to derrickman. Being way up there in the derrick tripping pipe was a blast. There were occasional days when the drilling was really slow and we weren't making much progress. That could get monotonous, but a lot of the time it was dangerous and hairy. I got banged and bruised up a lot, but that just went with the territory. Working offshore, I saw men's arms and legs get broken. I held a friend of mine after his foot got mashed off. Lots of stuff like that.

I dug the danger. Whenever a situation came up, a critical situation, and only one man could get in the riding belt and hang on a cable over the side of the rig and swing a hammer, that guy would be me. Give me a hammer, put me in the belt, and I'll "get her done."

When I first started out, I thought, Man, this is going to be one great job. Isn't it warm in the Gulf of Mexico during the wintertime? Subtropical, right? I soon learned when you're out on that water and it's 35 or 40 degrees, and the wind's blowing forty miles an hour, it is freaking cold. It's not like those rigs up in Alaska where the whole derrick is enclosed and they've got huge heaters. We never got any of those in the Gulf of Mexico. We were lucky if we had a tarp to keep the wind off us. Management seemed to have the same mentality that I had, that it's the Gulf of Mexico, how cold can it get? Well, pretty damned cold.

I had a wild brush with one hurricane in 1983. Hurricane Chantal hit Galveston, killed thirteen people, and did about $100 million in damage. Chantal may have only been a Category 1, but since it was a full-blown hurricane, they decided to fly everybody off the rig via helicopter—everybody, that is, but the drill crew. We were always the last ones off since we were in charge of chaining everything down, securing what was left on deck, making sure things were fastened down good and tight, and preparing the rig for the hurricane blast. That was our job.

There must have been about ten of us marooned on the platform when the helicopter pilot radioed and told us that the storm had gotten so bad that they couldn't fly anymore. Instead, they tried to get a workboat to back up to the rig. The crane operator was supposed to put us in a personnel basket and lower us down onto the deck of the boat. Those waves were the biggest I'd ever seen, and as they tried to back up to the rig, we were looking over the handrails ninety feet down to the water. Seeing all those waves crashing over the back of that boat, I remember saying to myself, "I think I'll take my chances right here if it's all the same to you, Lord."

The skipper of the boat radioed us that he had two feet of water in his galley and that he had to leave. We were stuck on the rig, which was fine with me. It was at that point that the company man, who worked for Texaco, freaked out. He ran into his office and closed the doors. Now, here's the guy who was supposed to be the company man. Our leader. He was scared shitless and locked up in his room, probably crying like a baby while the rest of us were wondering if the engines in the lifeboats had been serviced lately.

I'm a survivor, so I had my plan. I wasn't going to die out there in the Gulf. This hurricane wasn't gonna kill me. So I strapped on my life vest and went as high up as I could go—which was up to the wheelhouse on top of the living quarters where I used to sit, drink coffee, and play my guitar. It was Near-Death Experience No. 3 (or 4, I don't remember). I sat right in the middle of that little room, twenty feet by ten feet, thinking to myself, "If the rig starts falling to the left, I'm exiting stage right. If it goes right, exit stage left. Simple as that."

A few other guys and I sat in that room all night as the Global Marine jack-up staggered and swayed. The wind was so powerful, you could step outside around the corner, hold your slicker suit open, and lean into the wind at a forty-five-degree angle. It felt like I was flying.

What eventually sucked about Hurricane Chantal was that the next morning, after one big perfect storm passed and went on through, it was time to go back to work and unchain everything. Here we were, up all night long, and now it was time to get right back to work!

Working on drilling rigs instilled my faith in my future. The way I figured it, even if I had a weak mind, I still had a strong back; I could always earn a good living working in the oil industry. I'm not saying guys who work offshore or in the fields are stupid. I'm just saying that at the time, the oil fields were still the place where a man without a college degree could work his way into a good-paying gig, which was where I was headed. I stayed out there for six years, making damn good money. It would have only taken a few more years before I hit the six-figure mark. I could have been very comfortable and it would have been a great life. I was on the job site in the Gulf of Mexico, on a rig, and not stuck in some stuffy office.

But as you might suspect, the easiest and most sensible way isn't always my way. As much as I dug the danger and the hard work on the oil rig, I could still see another road out there that was just as crazy and unpredictable. Namely, playing country music for a living.

Chapter Eight

EVERY LIGHT IN THE HOUSE . . . OIL, WATER, AND LOTS OF WIND

HAD BEEN PONDERING OUR ENERGY AND ENVIRONMENTAL policies long before I recorded a song called "Every Light in the House Is On."

There's no denying it. We pollute too much. We should have cleaner industries with far less waste. We should develop alternative sources of energy. We should do everything we can to protect the natural environment. We should. We should. We should.

But we don't.

How ready are you for the lights to go out in the hospital emergency rooms and homes for the elderly? Or for there to be no gas for your car, no heating oil or natural gas for your home? Last time I checked, we were still extreme energy junkies. Batteries for iPods don't grow on trees. I believe the energy battle has three fronts: 1) reducing our consumption at home; 2) protecting our energy sources both on American soil and overseas; and 3) utilizing instead of hoarding our own natural resources.

Everybody knows we haven't built any new refineries in the United States since the 1970s. I'm pissed off at the oil companies about it just as much as everybody else, and I worked in the oil in-

dustry. I don't understand why they have not built any new refineries. Is it because nobody wants a refinery in their backyard? I don't
understand it. Why not lay a couple of hundred miles of pipeline
and build some refineries farther inland? Why do we insist on
building the refineries right on the coast where the hurricanes
come in and knock them down? If you moved them one hundred
miles inland, a hurricane would be just a strong wind by the time
it got to them. There are a few refineries inland, but we need more.

The environmentalists don't want any new oil refineries and
that's just fine for the big oil companies, who don't want too many
refineries to increase supply and lower prices. We're at a point
where even routine refinery maintenance shutdowns exacerbate
the tight gasoline supply-and-demand equation. It's a win-win
for the oil companies while the working person is screwed. Why
can't the government step in when there seems to be coziness between the big oil companies? Let's say Shell has a problem at one
of its refineries and its supply is down. How come Exxon's gas still
costs as much as Shell's does even though its own refineries are
running fine? What's the problem? That's baloney (that's a word I
never use). If Joe Johnson's widget factory is running fine, and my
widget factory breaks down, Joe will sell more widgets than me.
You take your lumps in business, but not in the oil business. Man,
those guys stick together.

Government price controls and taxing extra profits toe a very
fine line, in my opinion. The problem is that gas prices keep going
up and up and up, but they haven't hit that magic threshold yet!
That's all the oil companies are doing. They're trying to find out
where that ceiling is. They're trying to find out just how much we
are willing to pay, and so far, they haven't found it yet. More people are driving more cars and burning more gasoline and the price

keeps rising. So the oil companies shrug their shoulders and seem to say, "Hell, they must not care." Since our economy is apparently so stable and everybody has enough money to spend, nobody is willing to sacrifice. That's the key. As a society, we're unwilling to sacrifice our luxuries and our conveniences in order to conserve. We're so spoiled and so soft that we won't change until we're forced to, which will happen a couple of ways—either somebody turns off the tap or oil spirals out of our price range.

I feel bad for the kid who cuts my grass. He comes to me and says he's gonna have to charge me more per month. I know why and it's cool. It's gasoline, man, and I'm willing to give him fifty bucks more per month because he cuts a whole lot of grass on my farm. I'm still willing to pay him more because, like the rest of America, gas hasn't hit that ceiling yet where I finally yell, "No! I won't pay this. I'll do it myself."

All I know is what I've learned working in oil fields and on rigs at sea. Instead of having our energy supplies held hostage to religious unrest in other countries, we should be poking as many holes in the ground and seabed as we can right here at home. We've got to have some common sense about how we do things. Drilling technology, which I know a little about from studying it at Louisiana Tech and from a fair amount of hands-on experience, has progressed by leaps and bounds, thanks in part to concern over the environment.

Offshore drilling doesn't necessarily harm the environment. The rigs in the Gulf of Mexico serve as artificial reefs and are magnets for fish as the fishing boats try to get in as close to the rigs as possible. Even the stuff that gets dumped over the side of a rig is inert. The ocean is so inconceivably immense that—though I certainly don't recommend it—you could probably wreck an

Exxon Valdez in the ocean every week and it would not change the ecosystem. We're talking about parts per million. Trust me, there's a lot of blue water out there. I've seen it.

Speaking of oil tankers: The oil companies attempted to create some good PR when they announced they were going to "double-sided" hulls on all their vessels, but I think they should go further. Why don't they put huge sails on the ships so that when the winds are favorable they can throttle back those monster engines? They should do that, if for no other reason than that it would look cool as hell. I know that sailing vessels require much larger crews, but I believe they can afford it.

Another idea that might score some brownie points (and maybe even some carbon credits . . . shut my mouth!) for big oil might be nuclear power. The Navy does it. They should follow the Navy's lead and scrap the diesels.

There will always be internal combustion engines, though. I don't care how efficient solar-, wind-, and battery-powered alternative fuel sources are. A fully loaded eighteen-wheeler can't run on batteries. It's not gonna happen. You can't load enough batteries in a trailer to push the truck. We'll need something more potent to run that powerful an engine.

Still, the automobile manufacturers need to increase the fuel efficiency of their cars. The market will soon dictate that when gas reaches four and five dollars per gallon. We do need to keep some strategic reserves.

One place we should definitely be drilling is the Alaska National Wildlife Refuge (ANWR) and elsewhere in the Arctic. With the latest technology, we don't have to go right in on top of those reserves. If we want to protect and preserve the coastline, and give wildlife lots of leeway, we can go in from a long ways off and then drill sideways.

The argument against exploring for oil in ANWR is that it's not a big enough reserve, and it's environmentally dangerous. The estimates of oil supplies differ, but everybody agrees there are several years' worth of oil down there. There's never been an explanation of which parts of the environment are in danger. It's been said that caribou herds increase near oil pipelines because of the warmth of the pipes during the winter. It's like when I saw schools of fish around oil rig sites feeding on leftovers that got dumped overboard. Again, like nuclear power plants, the latest technological developments in oil drilling make spills a vast exception as opposed to the rule.

When we were drilling within a certain proximity to Mobile Bay in the Gulf, we had to have zero discharge. We brought in these big barges and pulled them up alongside the rig. All the discharge had to go into those barges off the rig. (I don't know what they did with those barges once they were full.) Today there are ways you can totally contain the discharge from the drilling process and store it. I don't know how feasible that would be in ANWR. It's a whole different game when you're talking about drilling on the North Slope of Alaska. Those are extreme conditions. But the rigs they use are totally enclosed so the workers aren't exposed to the subzero temperatures.

Back in the old days, as seen in movies like *Giant*, when drilling for oil first started the only way that you knew that you had a good well was when you had a blowout. The oil was shooting out over the top of the derrick and everybody rejoiced and danced in the oil rain, just like James Dean's character, Jett Rink. That doesn't happen now. We don't have blowouts anymore. They're very rare. Scientifically they know what's going on "down hole." They have geological sensors and rams in the wellhead that will close around the pipe and immediately seal it off. Then they'll get their pipes and lines hooked up and "bring the well in" in a controlled manner.

I truly believe we should explore for oil in ANWR. In Louisiana, there are oil wells all over the state. Geological surveys help oil companies select a location, where an acre is then cleared out in the middle of the woods. That's where they drill their well, set the tanks up, do their drilling, and then move on. The operation just sits there quietly, and in a few months, all the wildlife is back again. It doesn't seem to have affected anything long term. There's wildlife all over the place, and there are oil wells all over the place, too. Louisiana is still known as the Sportsman's Paradise.

I guess we would rather tangle with the Middle East than figure out how much of a reserve we have in ANWR and if it's worth tapping into. It's a political football and an opportunity for the environmental radicals to flex their muscles and make everybody believe that it would be a horrible and harmful thing to do, when in actuality it wouldn't.

Another thing we need to do is build new nuclear power plants. The newest plants are very safe, and they're far cleaner than any conventional fossil-fuel-burning power plant. You know I hate to praise the French for being sensible about anything, but like the Japanese, *they're* getting 70 percent of their electricity from nuclear power. We should be shooting for at least 40 to 50 percent of ours from our nukes.

I think we should have nuclear-generated power all over the country. They're hard at work on a nuclear waste disposal site right now inside Yucca Mountain in Nevada. They're building it so that we can store waste there until the end of time. By then we'll figure out how to shoot it off into space and really get rid of it. That's what we need to do—find some economical way to send our garbage into outer space. I'm serious. Just load a missile up with all our nuclear waste material, don't worry about orbits, and shoot it straight out to infinity and beyond. Wouldn't it be awesome if the first contact we have with an ET is a message that simply says, "WHAT THE HELL IS THIS CRAP?"

We still have this silly "no nukes" mentality left over from the *China Syndrome* and Three Mile Island days of 1979. How can we, as a nation, be on both sides of the energy issue? You want to stop global warming, but you insist on burning fossil fuels instead of carrying the torch for more nuclear energy. You can't take both positions. Nuclear energy is our way out. Solar is not practical. The sun only shines half the day, and on some days it doesn't shine at all. The wind blows, but it doesn't blow all the time. Still, I don't see any reason why every roof on every building shouldn't have solid solar panels. We *should* figure out how to do that, and cut down our energy costs on bright sunshiny days, and then sell the overage back to the utility companies. And why don't we floor our deserts with solar panels? Nobody goes there anyway.

I would like to build a house for my family that's as green as possible, but it's difficult. You know why? It's almost like buying a new computer. Whatever supplies I buy today will be outmoded five years from now and I'll have to throw it all away and replace it. I'm reluctant to make the investment in solar energy because I suspect in a few years they'll come up with something even better and more efficient.

Finally, we've got rivers all over the United States that are perfect for hydroelectric power, which produces zero waste and pollution. If some fish can't make it up the river to spawn, that's a pity. Now I'm all for fish getting laid, and I believe that's a problem we can solve if we put some good minds on it. Unfortunately if the Sierra Club saps have their way, we'll be back to scratching in the dirt with sticks looking for grubs to eat.

In my home state, the Tennessee Valley Authority (TVA) project helps Tennessee and the whole mid-South not only with energy, but also with flood control. This brings up a real sore point for me as a born-and-bred Louisianan: Hurricane Katrina. While we're spending billions upon billions to rebuild New Orleans, there's still danger ahead. Why? Well, I'll tell you. Katrina wasn't even a Category 4 hurricane when it hit. It was a strong Category 3. One of these days a Category 5 storm is going to come roaring off the Gulf of Mexico and turn all of New Orleans into a sad memory. They know it in New Orleans, which is why they have Beau Soleil parties when the sun is shining.

For all of the outcry over the mistakes at the federal level in the response to Katrina—and I'm not saying there weren't plenty of mistakes made at FEMA and elsewhere—they came after a string of bad decisions at the local and state level. If the authorities in New Orleans were even remotely competent, the human toll wouldn't have been anything like it was. Then to see that shameful looting and apparent dereliction of duty by the New Orleans Police Department, that was the real national black eye.

Being from Louisiana, I found the whole Katrina debacle personally shameful. At first I felt terrible for everybody who was affected by it. Then, the more I watched what happened, the more I found myself feeling embarrassed that I was from this incredibly dysfunctional state. From the governor on down, nobody knew what was going on, or what to do. What happened with Katrina was the classic breakdown in local, state, and federal leadership. You can blame it on miscommunication. You can blame it on anything you want to blame it on, but in reality, it was the abysmal leadership that was at fault.

The lowest point came when Governor Kathleen Blanco got on television and cried! As a strong leader, you *cannot* go on TV

and cry. When the shit hits the fan, we can't have our leaders crying. They've got to show strength. They've got to stand up and
lead. You can't become a blubbering bawler with makeup running
down your cheeks. That just doesn't work. Too many people are
looking to our leaders for hope, inspiration, and strength, and
that's what you have to project even if you don't know what the
hell you're talking about.

I watched Spike Lee's HBO documentary, the whole thing,
twice. It didn't take two viewings to recognize that he had an
agenda, and that he cherry-picked the people he wanted to talk to.
It was obvious that the program was slanted to prove one point,
which is that it was all the federal government's fault and that they
didn't respond quickly enough to the problem. However, you can't
discredit what those people said and saw, and how they felt. Like
I said, they too were victims of miserable leadership, from the
president to the governor and the mayor on down.

CAN ANYBODY ACTUALLY sit at the table with a straight poker
face and proclaim that global warming is a load of bull when the
possibility of whether it's true or not is starting to get scarier and
scarier?

I haven't paid close enough attention, until recently, but now I
believe there's indisputable evidence that this planet is warming
up. We cannot dispute that; it's factual. I recently went to Glacier
National Park, outside Kalispell, Montana. It was so beautiful, one
of my favorite places on earth. We did a gig there, so that afternoon we got a twelve-passenger van and me and the boys rode up
to Glacier National Park. Once we got up to the pass, we all
looked up and asked, "Where's the freakin' glacier?"

It's gone.

While there may be indisputable evidence that the planet is warming up, I'm not at all convinced that it's even partly our fault. Our planet has gone through several cyclical changes over time. Scientists have proved that. There's also evidence that warming happened regularly throughout the history of this planet. It's a naturally occurring phenomenon. It just happens. You have ice ages, and then the earth warms up again. A millennium later maybe the ice comes back. Maybe we're entering a warming trend that in no way can we be held accountable for.

They say that Mars is getting warmer, and nobody lives there.

Are we contributing to climate change? Probably, but I suspect to a minuscule degree. I can't imagine that we can create any more methane gas than all those big-assed dinosaurs that were crapping and farting all over the earth millions of years ago. I think the biggest part of global warming is nature and its natural cycles. Yes, I admit that we're part of it, but I strongly suspect that if we were all driving electric cars and weren't burning coal and oil, the planet would *still* be warming up.

Why is it that Americans are so guilt-ridden that we insist on shouldering all the blame? We always want to take on the wages of sin for the entire world, this time for the damned planet warming up. Are we the only offending portion of the planet screwing things up? Or are we just the earth's most guilt-ridden, hand-wringing, self-flagellating residents?

Global warming is the chic topic right now for the liberal elit-ists to harp on and beat us all over the head with. It's an issue where they *finally* feel they have the moral high ground, since they rarely have the moral high ground in almost any other argument they promote. By God, this time they feel they do, so they're screaming about it at the top of their lungs. Their hypocrisy knows no bounds. Why are the rich Hollywood insiders flying in private jets or taking helicopters instead of flying commercial airlines or taking the train like the rest of us? Why don't they stop doing that?

I'm all for alternative energy sources in order to do whatever we can to make the air cleaner, but clean air isn't my main motivation for energy efficiency. I just want us to get to the point where we can say to those idiots in the Middle East, "Look, we finally figured out how to burn our corn. Now you figure out how to eat your oil. Don't ever call us again. We're changing our phone number. Leave us alone."

RECENTLY I WENT TO the co-op farm supply store to buy a new battery for my tractor and the guy asked me if I brought my old battery in. I said no.

"Well, Trace, I have to charge you another eight dollars."

"You're charging me eight dollars because I didn't bring my old battery in?"

"Yeah, that's the new law."

Turns out in Tennessee, if you don't bring the old battery in for them to properly dispose of when you buy a new one, then you have to give them eight bucks. But I wasn't replacing a battery. I was buying a new one for a different purpose, and they still had to charge me so that I wouldn't try to throw an old one in the dump.

"If you bring the old battery in, Trace, we'll give you the eight dollars back."

It reminds me of the carbon credits system. I kind of understand it, but to me, it sets somebody up to become incredibly corrupt. The premise is to use the free market system to buy and sell antipollution chips. If I pollute more and you pollute less, then I can buy the carbon credits that you don't pollute.

Is this a government thing?

It started with the Kyoto Protocols. Now you can buy these carbon credits on an open market. If you clean up your factory, you're able to earn carbon credits, after which you can sell then on the open market to other polluters. Or, if you're an environmental organization, you can buy those carbon credits and retire them so no one can use them. So that's why Tony Soprano could dump asbestos in New Jersey? He bought up a bunch of carbon credits, and nobody gave a damn! It's like a get-out-of-jail-free card, and it's nuts. Don't worry about doing the right thing if you have enough money to buy the carbon points. You can go ahead and cheat. By the way, wasn't that Al Gore's defense for having such a high energy bill? That he bought carbon credits to balance out his excessive use of energy at home?

This whole concept seems ridiculous. Surely, some intelligent person in power will stand up and say, "Hey, what the hell is going on here? You all started doing this crap while I wasn't looking?"

It's like the kids coloring on the wall when Mom's not in the room. Isn't anybody minding the store in Washington, D.C.? They're letting these environmental wackos run scams. This is a good example of why I'm glad we didn't sign the Kyoto agreement. The idea was to use the free market as a way to give people incentives to cut their pollution. But what it really does is create this corruptible bureaucracy. If a factory in Pakistan emits an incredible amount of pollutants, instead of spending money to clean up their factory and figure out how to make it cleaner, they just pay a windfall sin tax in the form of carbon credits and keep going. Eventually it becomes corruptible currency.

EVER SINCE WE INVENTED the internal combustion engine, oil has been used as a weapon. For instance, oil defeated Adolf Hitler.

During the Battle of the Bulge, when Hitler was trying to stage an offensive, he ran out of gas. Eventually we defeated him. Actually, it was us and the lack of petroleum that defeated him.

I don't know that much about ethanol, but I suspect that it's a near wash, and that it takes as much power to produce as it will ultimately provide. Isn't it crazy to put eight gallons of diesel fuel in a tractor to plow a field that will make ten gallons of ethanol? We can make ethanol with corn or with sugar beets. In Brazil they weaned themselves from excessive gasoline use by using ethanol made from sugar. Unfortunately, we have an embargo from getting our ethanol from Brazil because we choose to make it with corn. Lemme see. Corn is grown in Iowa, the same state where one of the first presidential primaries is held, where politicians get a lot of traction for their contributions. Nowadays corn commodity prices are going through the roof because it's being used to make fuel *and* food. The price then skyrockets and a lot of poor countries that need that corn to feed their population now have to pay more for their food. While we feel better burning ethanol made from corn, we're actually making a negative impact on how Third World people live and eat. How crazy is that? What we need to be focused on is cellulosic ethanol, which produces energy from waste products such as wood chips, agricultural waste, grasses, cornstalks, hog manure, municipal garbage, sawdust, paper pulp, sewage, and other crap. Why are we not doing this? Is there, perhaps, a hidden agenda? Corn politics.

Unfortunately, without oil, the wheels of our country and our thriving economy would stop turning. In very short order there would be chaos and anarchy. And that's another part of the Big Picture most people don't think about. There is always some pacifist ideologue making his argument against war in another country by screaming that tired old catchphrase, "No blood for oil!"

Well, without oil, there is going to be blood flowing in the streets of *this* country. Ever seen the movie *Road Warrior*?

Until we develop alternative sources, we are going to be entirely dependent on petrochemicals for fuel, plastics, and more. It's all part of a cruel joke that God, in his infinite wisdom and strange sense of humor, played on us: giving all that oil to those psychos in the Middle East. But that's the way it is, and now we have to deal with them to keep the pipelines open. We need an alternative, and we're working on it, and someday we'll find it. I'm optimistic that our children's children will persevere and solve this problem in the end.

However, if you think those sons of bitches in the Middle East hate us now, wait until we stop sending them money for the oil we no longer need.

Chapter Nine

HONKY-TONK HIGHWAY

GOT INTO MUSIC, REALLY, BY ACCIDENT, BY HAPPENSTANCE. When I was working offshore on the drilling rigs, I'd take my guitar out there with me, work my twelve-hour shift, and then I'd go up and sit in the wheelhouse and play. It was quiet up there. I'd work from noon to midnight and then by one o'clock in the morning I'd take out my guitar and work on some new tunes I was writing or fiddle around with some old songs.

Pretty soon some of the guys I worked with started coming up there to hang out and hear me play.

"Hey, Trace! Play us a Haggard tune," or "Why don't you do that Hank Jr. song again?"

One of the guys at work wanted to hook me up with a band he knew from Lafayette, Louisiana. He told me to go check them out during my next two weeks off. At that time, when I was back home, I still used to go around to little jamborees and hay rides and get up with the house band and sing Don Williams and Haggard tunes. It was a hobby I enjoyed, dating back to when I was singing bass in gospel quartets.

During my next two-week break, I went down and met the guys from this bar band. They had just won the Wild Turkey Battle of the Country Bands in Lafayette and they were on their way to Dallas for the regional competition. After I sang a few songs that I had written, they invited me to come along with them to Texas and sing one of my songs along with three of theirs for the contest. I looked at my calendar. The Battle of the Bands fell at the right time, when I was off the rig, so I promised to perform with them in Dallas.

We walked onstage, and wouldn't you know, we won the regional round. After we won in Dallas, we arrived in Nashville to compete in the finals. Unfortunately, we choked and lost. But after the contest, we met up with one of the judges in Dallas, a guy named John Milam and his wife, Diana. They were booking agents, and after seeing us onstage that one time, John and Diana offered to send us out on the road. At that time, the name of the band was Speakeasy. Later on, we changed our name to Bayou since our new booking agents wanted a name that identified where we came from. Bayou was already a good functioning country band when I joined up. They just plugged me in as a singer and rhythm guitar player and we were ready to roll.

"We can book you no problem," said John. "You're good enough to work steady in Texas, New Mexico, and the Southwest circuit."

This got me to thinking. What if . . . ? This might be my shot. So in 1986 I took a six-month leave of absence from my job on the rig. I didn't exactly quit. I told the band, "I'll give it six months and let's see how this touring thing works out. If it doesn't gel, I'm going to have to go back to work offshore."

Well, we ended up staying on the honky-tonk circuit for three and a half years! It's amazing how the weeks and months flew by. We developed a loyal legion of club owners who hired us. There was a club in Dallas we played called Belle Star, and another in the Arlington area called Country Connection. Then we'd cross over to Fort Worth and do a gig at the Rodeo Exchange. After that it was on to Abilene to play at the Butterfield Junction. Next was some honky-tonk in Lubbock, then on to Albuquerque to play Cowboys. After that we'd swing back through Clovis and play Boot Hill. Sometimes we'd stop off in Las Cruces and "do time" at the Triple R. Then it was back to Dallas and on over to Jackson, Mississippi, to play for a couple of weeks in a club there. That's how it was; each tour spanned about six or eight weeks. We'd hit each club about every month and a half. That's how we built our modest fan base. We found that if we stuck with it, we could actually create a pretty good following. And we did. We'd gotten to the point where we were the second-highest-paid unsigned honky-tonk band in the Dallas/Fort Worth area. (Can't remember who was number one.) The money I brought in was just enough to keep me going and barely enough so that I could send a bit home to the little lady so she wouldn't think I was completely wasting my life away. Eventually, being on the Honky-Tonk Highway would cost me my marriage as my wife filed for divorce. She was lonely. I was lonelier. My travelin' was hell on our relationship.

The honky-tonk circuit was a grinding, tough way to make a buck. There were no luxury liners on wheels for Bayou. A lot of times we were driving down the road in a dilapidated motor home, a van, or a pickup pulling a beat-up trailer with a bunch of beat-up gear, praying the stuff still worked for the next date. Some weeks, nobody got paid because a speaker blew up or we had to replace a twelve-hundred-watt amp that conked out. We couldn't carry backup gear and we would have gigs lined up for the next month. Then the van would break down again. Or the engine in the motor home would sling a rod. A lot of the money was spent keeping everything going. Then there was our bar tab. During a show, sometimes we'd drink up our earnings. When it came time to collect, the night manager would give us the bad news at two in the morning.

"We don't owe you shit. See ya next time."

Playing bar gigs is the hardest low-level job in the music business. We were a traveling country jukebox, playing practically all covers. It was all about back-to-back-to-back current songs, with little talking onstage and no dead air in between tunes. Being a country band on the honky-tonk circuit meant that some of the contracts we signed in order to play the club had a clause that stipulated we had to know a set number of songs on the current Top Forty country radio countdown. That meant we had to rehearse like dogs every week, constantly adding new tunes in order to keep our set list updated. I have to admit, I worked a lot harder back then than I do now. Hell, I was singing four one-hour sets a night. Nothing personal, Randy Travis, but if I never have to play "On the Other Hand" ever again, that would be fine by me. In fact, I had to sing all of Randy's hits because I had the deepest voice. I also sang most of George Strait's stuff, and a lot of Garth Brooks, too. Whoever was hot at the time, I was singing their tunes. Every now and again I'd try to slip in one that I wrote. Nobody seemed to respond one way or another—which was both good and bad. Bad that nobody gave a damn. Good in that at least they didn't boo or throw things.

The gigs were ball-buster, Tuesday through Saturday engagements. Tuesdays were the absolute worst. One night when we opened at the Triple R bar in Las Cruces, there was us, the bartender, a pair of waitresses, and a couple of old drunks huddled in the corner. It came time for us to start our first set.

"I ain't playin'," I told the band. "Look, there's nobody out there, and I'm not doing it. Let's just sit here and wait until the place fills up."

By eight-thirty, the manager came out from the back and pointed at me. "Get on the stage, Bayou."

"C'mon," I pleaded. "There's nobody here. Those two fellas over there are so drunk they can't even talk to each other. So it's just us and you. Let's make it an all-request night. What do *you* wanna hear?"

Las Cruces on a Tuesday night. It was depressing being so far from my home and family. I'd ask myself, "What the hell am I doing here?"

But then we'd do a lot better over the border in Texas. It was back in the days before they raised the drinking age in Texas. During the mid-1980s, you could still get into a club if you were eighteen. When we played the Belle Star on the Central Expressway, all these gorgeous SMU college chicks would mob the place on ladies night. Yes, and they were wild, drinkin' types. It was a rough-and-tumble club. Later on it burned down.

I remember one night playing at Belle Star in Dallas when we were doing "Seven Bridges Road." The manager stood right in front of the brass rail at the front of the stage, arms folded, shaking his head. We were two feet above the dance floor.

"Don't do any more instrumentals!" he yelled up at me after the song.

"It wasn't an instrumental, dickhead. It was an a cappella number."

"Come to the office when you're done with this set."

I was boiling mad. I went to his office, closed the door, and started in on him.

"First of all, let's get something straight right now. When I'm up on that stage and I've got the microphone in my hand, I run this freaking club. You don't. If I say dollar shots of Cuervo at the back bar, you'd better start settin' 'em up or those cowboys are gonna burn this joint to the ground. When I've got that mic in my hand, I am in control. I'm running this club whether you like it or not." (Whiskey courage.)

"You weren't keepin' enough people on the dance floor," the club manager shot back.

At that point I'd had it. "Open the books and show me which band is sellin' the most liquor. Show me."

The manager opened the books. How much liquor sold during your performances determined not only how often you got booked, but how much you got paid. The closest band was five or six thousand dollars a week *behind* us in liquor sales. That's why Bayou was the second-hottest band in the region. The name of the game and the bottom line in honky-tonks: Who sells the most liquor?

Another time I wrecked a truck while hauling our gear on Interstate 635, north of Dallas. I was about to run out of gas and the roads had gotten a little icy. I spotted a gas station, so I tried to get off on the exit ramp, and as soon as I touched the brakes, my trailer jackknifed and came skidding around the side of me.

Now, our keyboard player, Randy, had rented an overhead projector from the library. He sketched "Bayou" on a clear overlay and projected it onto the trailer. One night we all got drunk and painted the name of the band on the side of the white trailer in big black letters.

Well, after the trailer jackknifed, I looked over, and there was "Bayou." At seventy miles per hour, a trailer is *not* supposed to be "by you," outside your side window. It all happened in slow motion. At that point, I was completely out of control of everything in life as I skidded toward the guardrail. All I could do was hold on to the wheel with all my might.

Our keyboard player was following me when he saw my truck had hit the guardrail. Then I flipped the truck not side by side but end over end. My front bumper would hit, then the back bumper, somersaulting down the interstate.

The front and back of the truck were totally smashed. The top of the cab didn't have a scratch on it. I remember coming to, lying in the driver's seat, with Randy crouched over the top of me, yelling,

"Are you dead? Are you dead?"

"Hell no, I ain't dead. Now get up offa me." Ha! It was my *fourth* brush with Mr. Death. I'd beaten the devil again.

The truck was totaled and I walked away with just a whiplash.

The trailer was found sitting in the middle of the road. After I hit the guardrail, the trailer rolled on down the interstate, went up the next incline, and rolled back down. The bumper of my truck was hanging on the tongue of the trailer. It's funny now, and it was kinda funny then. The next day we had a big laugh. The band gear was okay, that was the main thing. I was a little banged up, the truck was history, but the guitar amps were all okay, so we could play again tomorrow night. The show must go on!

We got into brawls on the road that should have been filmed to be believed. One night in Abilene I remember being onstage and looking out across the club and *everybody* was fighting! It was beautiful in a perverse kind of way. It was like something out of the movies. Cowboys out of control, arms and legs flailing, chairs, bottles, and shot glasses flying all over the place. The whole club was fighting and it was total chaos. I loved it, and we just kept on playing. We never did play behind any chicken wire, although we probably should have a few times.

The club Cowboys, in Albuquerque, was just as rough as that place in Abilene. Boot Hill in Clovis was an ornery honky-tonk roadhouse—many a boot landed on someone's rear end in that place. But the worst beating I ever took in my life was in Fort

Worth at the Rodeo Exchange. Kelly, the manager, and I were really good friends and Bayou played there once a month. We were practically the house band. We had a blast every time we came through town. It was a nonstop party from the time we rolled in until we staggered out, Tuesday through Saturday, and sometimes we'd play on a Sunday so Kelly could slide us some extra money. The place was packed every night.

One night after the last set, I went over to Kelly's house, where there was always a party goin' on. Lots of people had shown up afterward, and there was this really hot babe there. After we hung out together for a few hours, I sensed that we were about to get to know each other much better. But I was kinda suspicious of this chick, so I asked her outright, "How old are you?"

She told me the truth. She was much too young, seventeen years old.

So I said, "Get out!"

The next night I was up on the stage, and the same chick showed up at the front door. Kelly came up to the bandstand in between songs.

"Hey Trace, this girl at the front says she knows you. She doesn't have any ID. Will you vouch for her?" Kelly didn't remember her from the night before, but I knew she was trouble.

"I don't know her." And that was the end of that. Or so I thought.

After we got through playing that night, I went into the office where Kelly was counting out so we could settle up for the night. I was waiting on him because we were going back to his house for more partyin'!

"Man," Kelly said to me, "that girl sure raised hell when I wouldn't let her in. So I kicked her butt out. She said she was going to get her five brothers and come back and stomp our asses."

As soon as we got to Kelly's car, which was parked up against the building, a car pulled up behind us, and five dudes began piling out. Kelly got out, wondering what the hell was going on. He was a tough little guy, and boy could he fight. He jumped out of the car, cussing and carrying on. Then I saw the jailbait chick there with her five "brothers."

"Oh no!"

By the time I got out of the car, they'd already jumped on Kelly and were working him over. The first guy I grabbed was getting out of the backseat. I collared him, slammed him up against the car, and punched his lights out. But when I hit him, I thumbed him in the eye, which bent my thumb back and broke it. (I still have a knot on my hand from that night.) After I broke my thumb, another guy came around behind the car and clocked me right in the jaw. I didn't remember anything else after that.

When I came to, I was lying facedown. They had stomped me from the back of my neck to my heels, all down the backs of my legs. Kelly was leaning up against the wall, bloody. They beat the shit out of him, too. A few days later I was bruised black and blue from head to toe. It was dark that night. I wouldn't know any of them if they walked up to me today. All I remember was them saying, "We're from Oklahoma!"

I figured if that's what they did to me for *not* messing around with their sister, who knows what they would have done to me if I had?

All through my honky-tonkin' days, I held out hope that one night I would be playing in one of those clubs and some rich Texas oilman was going to walk in, hand me a stack of cash, and tell me, "C'mon son, I'm gonna make you a star."

Maybe it's happened that way before to somebody else, but it never happened to me. It didn't take very long until I was fronting the band. There were five of us: keyboards, lead guitar, bass player, drummer, and me, singing and playing rhythm guitar. I heard someone from Mercury Records came out one night to check me out, but who knows if that even happened. Anytime someone would come out to see us, I'd find out after the fact. Or maybe they showed up on one of those nights when a tray of tequila shots had just been delivered to the stage, and I was so hammered I couldn't sing straight and they just walked out.

At one point the guys in Bayou sat me down and had a come-to-Jesus talk with me about my wild ways. It was the first intervention that was ever pulled on me. But I wasn't having any of it at that time. I had assumed de facto leadership of the band by then. My feeble argument: If they can't take the heat, then get out of the damned kitchen. Drunk or stoned, this is the way I operate, and if you want out, there's the door. And that was it.

But that wasn't it. Being wasted all the time weighed heavy on my mind, and I knew the only way out was just to quit the band and get off the road.

A year or so later I hit bottom. I woke up one morning totally hungover. Still wasted, really. It was 1989. I slowly stumbled into the bathroom and propped myself up in front of the mirror. I remember vividly saying to the mirror image looking back at me, "Five years ago, I wouldn't have been caught dead hanging out with somebody like you."

I had sunk to that level. I was doing a lot of coke and meth in Albuquerque. Snorting crank in Jackson. Smoking weed in Louisiana. Taking X in Dallas. Drinking way too much everywhere else. I'd just woken up and done my morning ritual: Before I opened my eyes, I reached over the bed and felt around for that gallon jug of Cuervo, found it, grabbed the handle, spun off the cap, and then I turned it upright—all before I even got out of bed.

That was how I kick-started my day, and those are the depths to which I'd sunk while on the road constantly playing clubs. The Honky-Tonk Highway was killing me.

Looking at myself in that motel mirror and seeing a lowlife staring back at me was my personal epiphany. I couldn't live with myself anymore—and rehab wasn't an option because I had no money. "That's it," I said to that dude in the mirror. I gave my booking agent and the band two weeks' notice.

"But we have six months of dates on the books," the band said to me.

"Not with me. I've had enough."

I was going home, then back to work on the oil rigs. I'd paid enough dues and my honky-tonkin' days were over.

For a while, anyway.

Chapter Ten

LEGENDS, INFLUENCES, AND
NASTY COUNTRY SONGS

MY MUSICAL ROOTS RUN DEEP AND WIDE. WHEN I WAS A boy the only records on the stereo at home were country records. I first learned how to play guitar listening to my daddy's album collection. I wore out my father's copy of *Honky Tonk Heroes* by Waylon Jennings. That's how I studied the guitar. I learned all the songs off that record, plus other records by Don Williams, George Jones, and Merle Haggard, to name a few.

Hands down, Haggard was my favorite artist when I was first exposed to country music. It amazed me how the man could sing notes that were in the proper key, but they were notes nobody else would have thought to sing. In some weird way, they fit. I know he learned that style of singing from Lefty Frizzell, but Lefty was dead and gone by the time I came along. So Haggard was the first singer I heard singing notes that are in the scale and technically correct, but not that melodically obvious. Sometimes they barely fit into the structure of the song.

I've spent a lot of time studying his recordings. Haggard evokes a style in his singing that people who study music at Juilliard would find astute and clever. I've always dug how he would hit a seventh or a harmony note. Haggard is a living legend. I have some of my daddy's old Haggard albums framed on the wall in my barn—the old Capitol *Best of* albums. That's what I listened to when I was a kid, which inspired me to become a singer today.

I wasn't really exposed to other forms of music until I was older. I was pretty much into country and gospel until I started driving my own vehicle and buying my own music to listen to in my truck. As a teenager I was into the usual rock acts that are now considered "classic rock": bands with strong vocals like Foghat, Journey, Boston, Kansas, and Foreigner. I also liked Bob Seger, Atlanta Rhythm Section, Tom Petty, and the Eagles (and every Southern rock band known to man).

Even though I loved rock 'n' roll, I still listened to hardcore country. My tape case in my first pickup truck in high school reflected all my favorites. I enjoyed Southern-fried gospel quartets like the Inspirations, the Cathedrals, and the Florida Boys, and then I had the old standbys like Haggard, Hank Jr., Ronnie Milsap, and Waylon Jennings, along with .38 Special, Lynyrd Skynyrd, and Molly Hatchet.

Seeing live bands inspired me, too. One of the biggest bands in country to come along when I was a kid was Alabama. They were the first band I saw live. I drove all the way to Shreveport to see them. In my opinion, they helped bridge the gap between country music and Southern rock. Alabama had that country band format cookin' with the Creedence Clearwater Revival leanings, which was a big influence on me. You can trace the country and rock blend all the way back to the early roots of rock and rockabilly. Guys that are now in the Country Music Hall of Fame were often rock 'n' rollers, too, including Johnny Cash. Conway Twitty and Charlie Rich both started off as rock crooners. In the late 1970s, a few pop and rock bands went country—like Exile, that band from Kentucky. I like them a lot. I remember when "I Want to Kiss You All Over" went to number one in 1978. They sang in gospel harmonies and eventually drifted over to country.

I get accused of singing songs that are considered a little too sexy and suggestive. Let me suggest that you go back and listen to country music from twenty or thirty years ago and check out what Conway Twitty was singing about. Conway sang songs that I could never sing in public today. He had country hits with tunes like "Don't Call Him a Cowboy (Until You've Seen Him Ride)," "I'd Love to Lay You Down," or "You've Never Been This Far." Check out the lyrics. Really nasty stuff. Check out Charlie Rich's "Behind Closed Doors." Is that sexy enough? Alabama had a big hit on the radio in 1984 with a song called "When We Make Love." It could have been called "When We #$@&." That's really what that song was all about. I'm afraid that those kinds of songs had a profound influence on me.

Waylon's *Honky Tonk Heroes* shaped my music, look, and attitude in many ways. It's one of the greatest country albums ever made, which poses the question, why aren't there any honky-tonk heroes around anymore? I even love the album cover! It's a black-and-white candid shot with Waylon, his band, and songwriter Billy Jo Shaver sitting around an empty honky-tonk smoking and drinking beer. Waylon is stringing up a guitar with a wide grin on his face. They were all dirty, greasy, and long-haired. They looked like bikers, not hippies.

When I was in high school, in the late seventies and early eighties, it seemed like everybody that was cool had long hair. So, when I worked offshore and started singing in clubs, being a long-hair fit the life I was living, just like that photo on the cover of Waylon's *Honky Tonk Heroes*. Musicians looked like Waylon because that's how hard they lived their lives on the road. And that's how I was living my life, too, so I just let my hair grow.

Why can't we have record covers like that anymore? When they shot the cover for my album *Dangerous Man*, I wanted it to look funky and loose, kind of like *Honky Tonk Heroes*. It's funny, though. Nowadays I'll do a cover shoot with makeup artists, stylists, and wardrobe people hovering around me, while Waylon just sat there in a freaking beer joint and somebody snapped a picture. That's what I wanted. So we compromised. The *Dangerous Man* cover is a black-and-white photograph of me kicking back in a chair, looking serious with my game face on.

While I like the old music, I also like where country music is at right now. Country, to me, is the most inclusive type of music there is. I can go out onstage tonight and do a stone-cold country song and then throw in a Blackfoot-type rock song and the whole crowd will dig it. I'll break into the blues or I can do "Chrome," which is essentially a country rap song. Then for a little crunk we'll do "Honky Tonk Badonkadonk." Country audiences are far more accepting of different genres of music, whereas not many rock or pop singers can stand up and do a stone country song and get it played on pop radio. We can rock on country radio. And we do.

I believe a lot of the classic Southern rock bands from decades past would be considered country bands today. If those bands were getting signed today they would almost certainly be played on country stations and not rock radio or pop radio. Marshall Tucker? Country band. Charlie Daniels, a straight-ahead Southern rocker in his early days, now he's a bona fide country legend. The Eagles? A country band by today's standards. Classics like "Lying Eyes" and "Take It Easy" are pure country. The Allman Brothers? Today they would be a country band. They might argue that point, but if you listen hard, I think you'll find I'm right.

I think the reason country music sounds the way it does today, with its pronounced rock edge, is because of the producers. The top producers in Nashville right now are in my age group and, like me, they started hitting their stride in their late thirties and early forties. They grew up listening to the same music I did, bands like the Eagles, Alabama, Lynyrd Skynyrd, and the Allman Brothers, and Merle Haggard. They may be producing some twenty-three-year-old kid out of music school, but his music sounds like some of the music I used to hear on my FM rock stations. In addition, the songwriters in Nashville, who are really at the top of their game, are also in my age group, thirty-five to forty-five, and were heavily influenced by the same blend of country and rock we grew up on.

We all need legends and influences to look up to. I've had a chance to meet almost every legend I've ever wanted to. I got to meet Haggard and sing with him when I did a television show in 1998 called *Working Man: A Tribute to Merle Haggard*. The show featured a bunch of country singers like Alan Jackson, Emmylou Harris, Tim McGraw, and Wynonna Judd, all doing Haggard tunes onstage with Merle and his backup band. It was a great night and was one of the highlights of my career. I sang one of his early songs from 1967, "I'm a Lonesome Fugitive."

The first time I ever did a show with George Jones, I was his opening act in the late 1990s. He had no idea who I was, and after I had played my set, I stood in the wings to watch George do his thing. Toward the end of his show, his road manager came up to me and said, "Usually the opening act goes out at the end of the show and sings 'Rockin' Chair' with George. Do you want to?"

"Yeah!"

When I walked out onstage, George looked over at me and

kind of stepped back. At first I think he expected security to escort me off the stage. But since I had a microphone in my hand, he knew I was there to sing, and we did the "Rockin' Chair" duet together, in a sort of call and response way, which was awesome.

"My God," I was thinking as we were singing, "I'm out here with George Jones!" It didn't matter that he didn't know who the hell I was.

Ed Bruce was another one of my major influences. His biggest hits included the original version of "Mammas Don't Let Your Babies Grow Up to Be Cowboys," "My First Taste of Texas," and "Homemade Love." I was singing bass in a gospel quartet at the time, while performing some country stuff on my own during the weekends. One night I was watching the Grand Ole Opry on TV and Ed Bruce came out and sang one of those beautiful ballads with *his* signature rich, bass voice.

"Wow!" I thought. "I might actually be able to make it as a country singer after all."

Ed was such a pivotal influence on my career. When I finally had the opportunity to sit down with him, he actually came over to my house. We were originally going to write a song together, but it just ended up with me sitting there all night on the edge of my chair saying, "Come on, Ed. Sing somethin' else."

There have been a couple of times where I've been too shy to approach the really big stars. For example, one of the reasons I got into the music business was to meet Ray Charles. I was performing on a show called *The 100 Greatest Songs in Country Music* in 2003 for Country Music Television (CMT). He appeared on the show with me, Glen Campbell, Vince Gill, Kenny Chesney, and John Michael Montgomery. There he was right next to me. I was so in awe of him, I couldn't speak. After he sang his song, his handler was taking him to his dressing room. I desperately wanted to meet him. It was the perfect opportunity for me to excuse myself and shake his hand. But I choked; I didn't have the courage. So I just stood there in silence and let him pass by. I missed that one opportunity to shake Ray Charles's hand, all because I was too chickenshit and didn't want to bother him.

The same thing happened with Johnny Cash. I never got to meet Cash, either. I was in his presence a couple times, but was too awestruck by the Man in Black. It just didn't feel right. I didn't want to waste his time or impose on him with my babbling chatter. I wasn't worthy, so I chose to stand just close enough to catch his vibe and aura.

Sometimes it's enough just being a fan. It gives you an added perspective. When I do interviews on the radio and they ask me how I knew a certain song would be a hit for me, I say it's because first and foremost I'm a real country music fan! I listen like a fan. I react like a fan. If a song speaks to me, then I know that other people will dig it. I'm not so self-absorbed that I only sing songs that *I* think are cool. Being a good country singer is about *knowing* which songs the real country fans out there will relate to.

I'm a fan of most of the headliners (and co-headliners) that I've done shows and tours with over the years. The coolest part of the whole country gig has been the people I've met and idolized over the years and then having the chance to meet and sing with those people. Guys like George Jones. Merle Haggard. Waylon Jennings. Ed Bruce. Ronnie Milsap. Don Williams.

And speaking of legends, have you heard the story about the guitar player who dies and goes to hell? The devil shows him to a room where he's going to spend eternity, says goodbye, and closes the door. There sit Stevie Ray Vaughan and Jimi Hendrix, both on stools. Next to them is an empty stool and a solid gold engraved Les Paul guitar. Our guy sits down, picks up the guitar, tunes up, and starts to play. It's got the sweetest tone he's ever heard. Then he looks over at Stevie Ray and Jimi and says, "This is hell?"

Suddenly the door opens, and in walks Karen Carpenter.

"Okay, boys; let's take it from the top."

Chapter Eleven

COWBOYS AND RAMBOS IN THE WHITE HOUSE

'M INCREDIBLY FRUSTRATED WITH THE STATE OF AMERICAN politics. I've always voted Republican, but I'm fed up with the Republican Party. Sometimes they look as bad as the Democrats. If there were a viable third party, I'd seriously consider joining it.

My country, right or wrong; my family, right or wrong; but no political party or issue group has my unquestioning allegiance. I'm a lifelong member of the National Rifle Association, but I don't even toe the line for them. I don't march to their drumbeat. I march to my own.

For instance, I don't see a problem with a seven-day waiting period for somebody to get a weapon. That's not unreasonable. It's not infringing on my constitutional right to keep and bear arms. It just gives law enforcement a chance to make sure that I'm not John Hinckley before I get the weapon. I don't have a problem with that. I also don't have a problem with an average American not being able to own an assault rifle or a machine gun. Would I like to have one? Yeah. Do I really need one? It'd be fun. But I don't need that, or a missile launcher.

—

MY QUARREL WITH the Republican Party started relatively recently. For instance, once the war in Iraq started up, I disagreed with President George Bush on his tax cuts. True, the cuts stimulated the economy, but to extend those cuts, while we're spending money on the troops in the Iraq War, seemed irresponsible. Yet another example of America's unwillingness to sacrifice at a time when we should, when we need cash pumped into the coffers to keep this badass military machine rolling. Sure, I benefited from those tax cuts, but it wouldn't have hurt me if they hadn't extended that tax break.

I only wish more people in government, Republicans as well as Democrats, were freer thinkers instead of just voting along party lines. What an exercise in futility the whole legislative process has become in this country! After a politician wins an election they start collecting money for the next campaign. That's what it's about. Serve your term. Don't make anybody mad. Don't ruffle any feathers. Don't do anything that might be considered controversial or innovative. Don't piss off the base. Play it safe until the next election.

If only we had a president with the ability to stand up and relate to us as intelligent human beings. It may take another actor—like a Fred Thompson—who has the kind of skills to communicate clearly. I'd like to have a president who could stand before the American people and be straightforward. Give us a little history lesson behind some of your decisions. Then give us the plan. President Bush has not done that.

I don't understand why lawmakers are so afraid to talk straight with their American constituents. Tell us what we need to do in order to get things done. Don't be afraid to ask us to sacrifice if that's what it's going to take to win the war. Spell it out plainly instead of kowtowing to the polls and focus groups, telling us what you *think* we want to hear. Lead! And who are these idiots who get polled anyway? They've never called me!

Campaign finance reform would be a good place to start, but I don't have a clue how that's ever going to be accomplished. I can't imagine anything's ever gonna get done on that front because politicians will always create loopholes and escape hatches when it comes to taxes and money and especially political contributions.

Meanwhile, the Republicans and Democrats do little more than posture from across the aisles. It would be great if we didn't have all these people living on the public payroll in Washington, D.C. Government should be as small as possible, but strong enough to make decisions as a society and to solve problems we as individuals can't. That's what the politicians should be concentrating on. That's what they're elected to do.

But these guys don't have their eye on the sparrow. I swear, you come out of a meeting with your duly elected representative and you find yourself thinking, Does there *always* have to be a fat campaign contribution on the table, or under it, before they commit to any action?

In my experience, it doesn't necessarily have to be anything controversial in order to run into government indecision and gridlock. For example, my five-year-old, the second-youngest of my five daughters, has severe food allergies. This is a much bigger problem than it used to be. We must be doing something to our babies to make so many of them allergic to nuts, dairy, wheat, and a whole lot of other foods that should be good for them. These allergies contribute to asthma and other serious health problems.

If these kids eat the wrong thing, they can die from anaphylactic shock. Benadryl is the "go-to" drug for parents like us and must be readily accessible at all times. You also must have a shot of epinephrine ready all the time in case there's an emergency. When the children are really little, you worry that the epinephrine will be more than their hearts can handle. Fortunately, my wife and I have never had to give our daughter a shot, but we have had to rush her to the emergency room a few times.

As a result, my wife and I have been working to raise awareness of the problem with a great group called the Food Allergy and Anaphylaxis Network. Because of my semisuccess as a performer, I participated in some meetings with politicians. All we wanted to do was initiate some public service outreach by the U.S. Department of Education to school systems around the country: have the department send out basic information about dealing with kids with food allergies, including first aid measures and alternative school lunches and so on. We're not trying to set a single national policy that all school systems have to follow; we're not trying to create more bureaucracy.

The response was ridiculous. Of course, the first thing the politicians you're visiting say is that they share your concern. It was just like being on *Oprah*. But after that, they start hemming and hawing about how this is a delicate issue and how they're gonna have to consider all sides. What issue? What sides? They're on autopilot, saying the same thing they say to everybody except the people with the big money. That's when I begin to have a hard time controlling myself. In my eyes, there are only two sides to this particular issue: the side with the kids that are still breathing, and the side with the kids that aren't.

I LONG FOR the good ol' days when Republicans were Republicans. Conservatives like me loved Ronald Reagan. We wax nostal-

gic about his optimism and how he returned the country to prosperity and broke the Soviet empire. We all remember the famous
"Morning in America" election commercial that redefined conservatism and his "Mr. Gorbachev, tear down that wall" speech. But I
became a *real* fan of Ronald Reagan after he bitch-slapped
Muammar Gaddafi.

That's when Reagan called Gaddafi the "mad dog of the Middle East" and in 1986 sent bombers into Libya, blew up his house
in Tripoli, and ran a missile right into the tent where he used to
sleep. The day that Reagan was sworn in as president, the Iranians
turned the hostages loose. They knew what was about to happen,
there was a new cowboy in the White House, and somebody was
fixin' to get their ass kicked. After four years of Jimmy Carter, we
finally got ourselves a freakin' Rambo in the White House. This
guy was not going to take any shit from anybody.

Although I voted for George W. Bush, I haven't been a huge
fan lately. I'm disappointed in him. I don't know what happened.
He seems to have lost the fortitude to do what it takes to get the
job done. The cowboy spirit he had in his first term is gone. I
think his heart is in the right place, and I think he means well
and that he is a good-hearted soul, but maybe he just got some
bad advice and wasn't willing to risk the Republican Party's future on what needed to be done to get the party back in the game.
Until the Republicans come back home, the Democrats will continue to gain ground by running conservative-Republican-like
candidates as opposed to the usual cadre of left-wingers and tree
huggers.

I grew up in an evangelical environment. They're a large voting
flock, no doubt about it, but I don't see this huge so-called Moral
Majority conspiracy where the pastor of each church gets his
weekly memo from the White House telling him what he needs to

talk about and which positions to take. If you ask me, it's all pretty cut and dried.

Which party do the gay activist extremists belong to? The Democratic Party.

Which party do the pro-choice people overwhelmingly belong to? The Democratic Party.

Which political party do members of the ACLU belong to? The Democratic Party.

Anti-gun, pro-welfare, anti-prayer, pro–illegal immigration . . . That's enough!

Evangelical Christians are said to vote overwhelmingly Republican. So what? Maybe it's the party that most closely reflects what they feel and believe. The only reason evangelical Christians are being vilified by Democratic pundits is that they're *perceived* as a powerful voting block. It's seen as a movement today, whereas back in the 1940s and 1950s, nobody even thought about the religious right. It wasn't an organized thing. The last time I checked, voting was an act of privacy. Who really knows how Christians vote? People can surprise you.

It was *Roe v. Wade* that single-handedly created the so-called religious right. Instead of making abortion a federal privacy issue, the Supreme Court should have kicked the *Roe v. Wade* question back down to the appeals court and let it remain a state issue as to whether individual states wanted to make abortion illegal or legal. Just like gambling laws. That way, we could have avoided decades of division and confrontation.

Being a parent, you never want to see your children indoctrinated before they're mature enough to be able to process their own information. I can be tolerant of opposing views. You can believe and do whatever you want and I won't raise hell or get in your face about it. It's only when someone tries to indoctrinate my children before they're mature enough to make their own decisions. Now that angers me. That's the problem I have with the *Heather Has Two Mommies* crowd. Let my kids be kids until the time comes when they can digest social issues and reach their own conclusions—conservative, liberal, or somewhere in between.

As a conservative, I'll probably continue to vote Republican mainly because the alternative still freaks me out. But I'm not happy with my party. They're not serving our interests. They're not fighting the good fight. How could a party have been in charge of the House and Senate and have a favorable majority in the Supreme Court and still not get things done? It just doesn't make any sense to me.

I'm also pissed off about the party's stand on immigration. Illegal immigration is the big issue with me because it comes down to the law. And the law is very clear. All we're asking our government to do is uphold it. Yet they won't do it. Illegal immigration was a big issue in the 2006 midterm elections and will become an even bigger issue in the upcoming presidential election. The Republicans are going to learn the hard way how the American public (and legal immigrants) feel about this issue because there is a huge group of conservative voters out there like me who are incredibly frustrated.

In the end, the Republican Party needs to do more than motivate people to go to the polls to vote *against* something or somebody. Negative energy is not going to work for the new conservatives in charge of rebuilding the Republican Party. The party needs to give people like me a *positive* message, as Ronald Reagan did. Give us someone who excites us. Give us hope and make us feel optimistic. If we voters don't have an inspiring reason to go to the polls, then the people are not going to take the time and effort to stand in line and put this country back on the right course.

Chapter Twelve

THE BIG "WHAT IF"

WENT BACK HOME TO LOUISIANA IN 1989 TO TRY TO PATCH my marriage back together, but it was just not working. I already had two daughters, Tarah and Sarah, and a wife who was so sick of me that she didn't want to try anymore. That relationship was done. It shattered me, broke my heart. I guess I really broke my own heart because it was mostly my fault. Three and a half years of playing around on the honky-tonk circuit took its toll. I was disappointed in myself that I let my drinking get to the point where it affected my family. I had tried to stop drinking, and I would go through periods where I might abstain for a long period of time, but I'd always start back. I didn't think I was an alcoholic then. Now that I look back, I most certainly was.

After I got off the honky-tonk circuit, I called my old company, Global Marine, and my old boss, to see if I could go back to roughnecking. They said to come on. So I went back to work offshore. Only this time, going back out to the Gulf was terrible for the first six months or so. After years on the road playing music and drinking, I was out of shape. I just couldn't hang. I wasn't the man I was four years before when I'd left. But I worked myself back into it.

While I was still trying to make my first marriage work, I was offshore when I suffered another accident. I practically sliced off my left little finger opening up a bucket of pipe dope. That Buck knife was sharp, and when it slipped I severed all the tendons in my pinky. It was just hanging off my hand backward. It reminded me a bit of the time I almost lost my nose after slamming into that school bus. I had to sit on the rig for three or four hours before the helicopter got there to take me to the hospital onshore. We didn't have a medic stationed aboard the platform. The only thing that scared me about my finger was that when it happened, I immediately feared that my guitar-playing days were done. When they permanently set my little finger, I told them to make it so I could hook it around the neck of a guitar. Even today I still can't reach up the neck to make certain barre chords, so that makes me a three-fingered guitar picker.

They airlifted me to the hospital in Port Arthur. When I got there, I had to call home to tell them I was laid up. I phoned home and my mother-in-law answered and informed me that my wife had checked into rehab the day before. I lay in the hospital for three days sick with worry, going out of my mind, trying to figure out what was going on with my family. Finally, and I'll skip the needless details, the marriage ended and I had sole custody of two little girls, ages one and four.

A little while later, I met another girl from Springhill. With Springhill right on the Arkansas line, that's where I hung out to let off steam, it being a bigger town up the road. That's where the movie theaters, burger joints, beer joints, and liquor stores were. So, I met this chick there named Julie. She was divorced like me, and Julie had a great steady job and loved my two girls, so one weekend we flew to Lake Tahoe and got married. I remember the preacher who performed the ceremony was drunker than Otis Campbell. He called me Julie and my new wife Trace.

Not long after I settled down with Julie, I got a call from John Milam, the guy who booked Bayou in the clubs. I had just hit thirty and had been out of music for three years. He had just relocated from Dallas to Nashville himself.

"Trace, are you still singing?"

"Man, I don't even sing in the shower," I said, which disappointed John. "I'm done with all that."

"Well, one of these days, you're going to have to look at yourself in the mirror and ask the question, 'What if?'"

"What if what?"

"What if you'd really gotten serious about your music? Trace, you gotta throw down the pom-poms and get in the game, son."

"What are you talking about?"

"You need to be in Nashville. Remember all those years when you were hoping someone might discover you playing in those Southwest clubs? You always wanted to be a country singer. Well, the factory where they make country singers is in Nashville. That's where you need to be."

It made perfect sense. Deep inside, I still hadn't completely shaken the music bug. I missed singin' and pickin'. I talked it over with my new wife. She was game for us to relocate.

We moved to Nashville in 1992 and settled in quickly. I didn't move there as a desperate musician dying to get signed. After my dues-payin' years on the Honky-Tonk Highway, I was more level-headed than that. This time I took a blue-collar route. I started working construction, pipe fitting, out at DuPont. I was a fitter's helper at first, learning how to fit pipe. The intensity of the work wasn't nearly as hard as roughnecking. In fact, it was a pretty easy gig.

I didn't roll into Nashville with the mad hunger and burning desire to be a star. I didn't immediately run out and find pickers to put a band together. After we moved in, my wife opened up an office selling insurance. While I was working, I took my time and eased back into the music business. I gathered together some pickers, with the help of the Milams, and we started rehearsing in the garage. This time I had myself a by-God garage band, and after a few weeks we got a gig at a little club outside of town called Tillie's and Lucy's. It was in a community known as Hermitage, about ten miles east of Nashville. When I say little club, I mean little. Tillie's couldn't have held more than a couple of hundred people.

I scouted out the place and I couldn't believe we had to audition for the gig, and that we actually had to go down one afternoon, set up our gear, and play for this lady, Tillie, to see if we were good enough to play in this little hole-in-the-wall old club. I guess that was a testament to how much talent was crawling around Nashville. But the *real* testament was when she told us how much she was going to pay us per night. Two hundred a night for a five-piece band! Forty bucks a man, ten dollars an hour. My reaction, especially after playing the honky-tonks for decent dough, was shock.

"Whaaaaat? I'm not leaving my house for that much money."

"Then we'll get somebody else to do it," Tillie said firmly. "And somebody else will."

I discussed the situation with the guys in the band. They had been in town long enough to know that in Nashville, there are people who will basically play for free in hopes of getting discovered. If you want to earn a living playing clubs, I suggest you go somewhere besides Nashville. Around every corner lurks a guy or gal dying for a record deal who will sing for free for four hours a night. A tip jar and a guitar.

"Dude," my guitar player told me, "that's how it is here. It's the going rate. She's not trying to lowball us."

I eventually came around, and our gigs at Tillie's (only four miles from my house) worked into a situation where we kind of became the house band playing Fridays and Saturdays. Soon I started meeting people. Now they call it networking. To me it was still honky-tonkin'. Somebody introduces you to this person who knows that person who needs to come out and see you. Since I didn't come to Nashville to hire studio pickers and cut demos or play free showcases, I figured if anybody wanted to hear me sing, I'm easy to find. I'm playing at Tillie's, this little beer joint just outside of town. Come on down and hear what I do. For a little extra dough, and to feel more relaxed in a studio, I was also singing demos for a guy who also lived out in Mount Juliet. At thirty or forty dollars a tune, I sang mostly really bad songs in a studio set up in the dude's double-wide trailer house.

I also played all kinds of strange, live, casual gigs. One night we were playing covers at a Realtors' convention at the Music City Sheraton off Briley Parkway. That's when a girl named Rhonda Forlaw came into my life. A friend of the wife of a producer friend I was working with had invited her to see me. Rhonda was working for Arista Records as a publicist. Seeing me that one time impressed her enough to drag Tim DuBois, president of Arista Nashville, to come out and hear me at Tillie's. It wasn't a staged formal showcase or anything like that. It was just a regular gig with my weekend-warrior beer joint band. After Tim came out and heard me, he handed me his card. I guess I was supposed to have my secretary call his secretary. We were going to "have lunch" that next week.

I went back and played for Arista again, and they gave me what is known in the entertainment business as a development deal. That is, a small budget to record some demos so they could figure out if I had enough talent and potential for them to sign me to a real record deal. This time I was wise and savvy enough, thanks to a great attorney, to put a time limit on it. I was thirty-two years old and felt like I was getting a big musical break, but I wasn't going to let anybody tie me up indefinitely "in development." My new attorney, Stephen, advised me to give them six months.

So now the Nashville music clock was officially ticking away, except there was danger on the horizon. A few days after I signed my development deal, something big—and deadly—happened. It was my closest brush with death, yet.

Chapter Thirteen

ON THE WRONG END OF A .38

HATE BLAME GAMES AND I DON'T THROW PITY PARTIES. Life is messy. When you fall down, you pick yourself up and go on. Don't waste time trying to pin the blame on somebody, even if life has dealt you some rotten breaks. Life has thrown me some hellacious curveballs, stuff that would make for a dandy pity party on the *Oprah* show. But life has also given me plenty of blessings and epiphanies.

For example, I am without a doubt an incurable alcoholic. Now I could blame that on my genes, my individual biochemistry, my childhood, my career ups and downs, and all the other excuses people use. But I choose to drink, or I choose not to drink. Having the disease of alcoholism is not like somebody holding a gun to your head and ordering you to drink. You have choices and the chance to wipe the slate clean.

For a long time I chose to drink, and a lot of unpleasant things happened as a result. Like what was happening with my second wife, Julie, when I was struggling to make it in Nashville as a professional musician and still keep my day job. We had been married about three years, and she had reached the end of her rope with my drinking. I wasn't in rehab or anything, but I was trying to manage my drinking and abstain as much as possible.

It was Presidents' Day, February 21, 1994, and I had the day off from work on my construction job. We'd just had a huge ice storm and there were broken limbs that had fallen down all over the yard. I had spent all day with a chainsaw cleaning up the mess.

To have some company, I'd gone down to the convenience store and bought myself a case of beer. I'd been drinking beer all day, happily working away in the yard. As far as I was concerned, no harm, no foul. I wasn't bothering anybody. I was in my own yard. Yeah, I was working with power tools, and yes, that's most definitely irresponsible and not a good idea, but, hell, I wasn't driving drunk or doing anything stupid that would endanger another person.

My wife got home that evening from work and when she smelled the beer on me, she exploded: "That's it. Get out of this house. I don't want you here anymore." This was just another of the many volatile arguments I'd had with Julie.

Well, my two daughters (now five and eight) from my first marriage were upstairs asleep. So I told Julie, "I'm not leaving here without my kids. Those are *my* kids. So if anybody's leaving right now, it's gonna be you."

I left the room and went to the bathroom. When I came back out and walked into the kitchen, the next thing I knew my own wife was pointing a .38 pistol at me. Then I did the stupidest thing I'd ever done in my life. I turned into Captain Redneck. I decided that I was going to disarm the lady.

I stuck my left arm out toward her, and to scare her I said, "Give me that goddamn gun before I take it away from you and beat your brains out with it."

That turned out to be not only the wrong words, but my last words. She pulled the trigger, and the bullet went through my left lung, through my heart, through my right lung, and out the other side. It was what my hunting buddies and I call a "kill shot."

The impact knocked me down onto the linoleum. I don't recall much, but I remember getting up and staggering down three steps into the den where we had just put down some brand-new Berber carpeting. I don't know where the hell I thought I was going, but in a moment of absurd shock and awe, I thought, "If I bleed on this new Berber carpet, she might shoot me again."

So I stumbled through the den and off to the back of the house where there was an atrium-like room. We called it the Florida room; it had plants and a tile floor. I thought, "This'll be good, I can bleed here." Before I passed out, I could feel the cool tile on my face. That was my last conscious memory.

Strangely, when I got shot, it didn't really hurt. I'm sure it hurts a lot more if you get shot in the leg, but my gunshot was so severe, my body immediately went into protection mode. I didn't really feel anything. When a bullet goes through two chambers of your heart and both of your lungs—and it essentially goes in one side of your chest and out the other—your body and mind does a beautiful thing. In order to protect you, it just shuts down. You feel nothing. I did feel pressure on my chest, like somebody was standing on top of me, and I couldn't catch my breath. The only time I started feeling pain was when I was in the hospital recovering, trying to come around. The recovery process hurt like hell, but the actual bullet wound, the shot, didn't really hurt that much.

We were living in Mount Juliet at the time, like I said, not far from Tillie's. My wife had called 911 and the ambulance rushed me around the corner to a church parking lot where a LifeFlight helicopter had landed and was waiting to fly me to Nashville.

The thing that really creeps me out is that I remember being loaded into the helicopter, even though I was out of it at that point, but I don't remember it from the perspective of lying on the stretcher. Instead, I saw an aerial scene of me being loaded into the chopper before I was flown to Vanderbilt Medical Center. I attribute my survival to Vanderbilt's LifeFlight. Their emergency room trauma team is as good as any on this planet, and for that I am grateful. I figure any place that teaches doctors to be doctors is a good place to end up after getting shot. If I had been back in Louisiana, fifty miles from the nearest hospital, I would have been a dead man, no question.

My parents started the five-hundred-mile trip to Nashville as soon as they heard what had happened. Several of my close friends in town were there immediately, including John and Diana, Mark and Stacey, and Big Joe and his wife, Kat. The doctors held little hope that I would survive and told my family and friends to go in and say goodbye.

When the surgeons put me back together, while they patched the holes on the outside of my heart, they didn't go into the septum and patch that hole. I guess they plugged me up first and maybe then figured, "If he lives, we'll go back in and do the rest."

After I spent several days in the intensive-care unit they decided that I could be moved to a private room. As I started getting a little better, Vanderbilt University medical students were lining up outside my door because they'd never seen or heard a deviated heart septum, which apparently I had, in an adult. You hear it sometimes in babies that are born with a hole in their heart, but you never hear it in an adult. It makes this weird heartbeat noise—"bish-too, bish-too"—as the blood travels between the two chambers.

I was in the hospital for a month or so. At first I just had oxygen on a little nose clip. Then after a couple of weeks, they came in and put the entire mask over my face and turned up the air. I was lying there thinking, "Shit, they're just gonna let me lie here and die."

The problem was that my left lung wasn't draining the fluid, so I was basically drowning. Then they had to cut me open again from the back and go in and clean that stuff out.

After that, I started to recover a little faster. I've always tended to be a little accident-prone in my life, and as I always say about my misadventures, "It probably would have killed a normal man." When I woke up with a big tube down my throat, the first person who came into the ICU to visit me was our keyboard player, and my friend, Billy.

"How you doin', T?" Billy asked me.

"Probably would have killed a normal man," I repeated, and his laugh did me good. I had survived my *fifth* near-death episode.

The recovery took several months. I caught a staph infection and I had to take vancomycin, but I couldn't take it through my arms because it kept burning the skin off. They had to put a Hickman catheter straight into my heart. I kept that going for a couple of weeks, and twice a day I'd have to hook up to a big sack of vancomycin. But that stuff also killed all the good bacteria in my stomach, so my stomach cramped constantly. Soon I couldn't eat, and I lost so much weight I looked like I was living in a concentration camp. Mr. Skin and Bones.

I was in good physical condition and was tough enough to have made it through the initial gunshot. I lived through that, but then I started having doubts, like are these sons of bitches just gonna let me lie here and die? Before I went into surgery to fix my lung problem, I wasn't so sure. But when I went in for my second open-heart surgery, because the hole in my septum wasn't healing, that's when thoughts of mortality *really* streamed through my mind.

They were going into my heart. It wasn't like they were digging cartilage out of my knee. I said to myself, "This could be it, Trace. *Happy trails, hoss.*"

After they told me I had to have the second open-heart operation to patch the hole in my septum, I told the doctor, "Dude, I don't want to go through all that again." The recovery from my first trauma surgery was intense. Man, they don't play around. They just cut you open, go right in, and it's not gentle. They're working fast, and they're not so concerned about tearing stuff. But the doctor was adamant: "We have to go back in there and patch that hole in your heart."

"Let me ask you something, Doc. How long would I have if you didn't operate? Isn't there a chance that it might heal itself up? How long would I live, if you didn't do it?"

"Maybe five years."

That was enough to convince me. Third time better be a charm.

That was in 1994. The shooter, my second ex-wife, got remarried, and I was happy for her. Nothing happened to her legally for shooting me, mostly because of my own testimony. When the police detective came into my hospital room to take my statement, he asked me, "What happened? Did you hit her?"

"There was none of that. It wasn't like that. I just told her, 'Better give me that pistol, or I'm gonna take it away from you and beat your goddamn brains out with it.'"

"So you were just trying to scare her, you weren't really going to do that?"

"I just wanted her to give me the damn gun."

At the time I was saying all this, they were giving me about as much morphine as one body could handle, mostly I think because they really didn't believe I was gonna make it. I was "off the hook" when the officer came in and took my statement and I told him the absolute truth. I probably still could have pressed charges, but when I finally got home from the hospital, my attorney and I weighed the options. This was around the time O. J. Simpson killed his estranged wife and her friend. (You know he did it.)

My attorney said, "Look, your wife's going to get on the stand and cry. You *will* be portrayed as the big mean ogre. She was scared you were going to kill her. And with the mood of the country right now with this O.J. case, it ain't gonna be good."

"Can't you just get me a good, clean divorce, and get this over with?"

"That we can do."

So I forgave my second wife for shooting me because I refuse to believe that she was actually trying to kill me. She was probably trying to scare me off and get me out of the house—until, in that one insane moment, things got out of hand.

Who's to bless and who's to blame? It would be crazy to pretend that we weren't both to blame for what happened. That's why I hate to see all those daytime self-help television shows that encourage people to blame everybody but themselves for their problems. I also have a problem with people who peddle this fantasy about how, after you come close to death, every day is a gift and all the flowers smell sweeter and the food tastes better and all that kind of stuff. I've had several near-death experiences, and that's all true—for a little while. But you soon forget and go back to being how you were before, trudging through life and trying to figure out how to get through another day.

Being shot in the heart was a weird sort of gift, though, because it brought me closer to Rhonda. At the time we were just friends and she was trying to help me get a record deal with Arista Nashville. She went out on a limb for me. Now, there I was, shot like a dog. Yet she came to the hospital room and brought me a little basket with purple African violets in it. I know it sounds funny, but those purple flowers and that simple act of human kindness really helped me pull through. She placed them on a shelf in my room so I could always see them. At the time, luck was the least likely way I would describe my situation. But when Rhonda came up to my hospital room and brought that little basket with the purple flowers, it was one of the luckiest days of my life.

Chapter Fourteen

BASS VOICE THAT CUTS LIKE A TENOR

T WAS 1994. I FIGURED THAT GETTING SHOT PRETTY MUCH ended any hopes of getting a record deal with Arista, but Rhonda came to see me in the hospital and assured me that when I got better, we'd try again.

Once I got out of the hospital, I got better, slowly but steadily. Six months later I required another surgery to put a patch over the hole that was still in my septum, the dividing wall between the right and left sides of my heart. After that, I really began to heal physically, mentally, and even creatively. I started singing again. By the end of 1995, almost two years after the near-fatal shooting, I finally got back into decent enough shape so that it was okay for someone to come hear me sing again at Tillie's. By that time, Rhonda and I had become much closer friends and had started dating.

One night I went to pick up Rhonda at the Nashville airport. She was flying in from Dallas after doing some fund-raising benefit. A fellow named Scott Hendricks was on the plane with her and it just so happened that he had just been named the new president of Capitol Nashville. Rhonda introduced me to him while we were standing around the baggage carousel waiting for her, per usual, fourteen pieces of luggage for a two-day trip. Then she invited Scott to come out and hear me sing that weekend at Tillie's. He agreed, and I remember thinking, "Yeah, right."

But I was wrong. That weekend, sure enough, Scott showed up at Tillie's as promised. I got up and played my first set, put my guitar down, turned around, and there was Scott, right in my face, standing on the stage in front of me.

"I'll give you a record deal."

That's all he said. No "Let's talk." No "Let's do lunch." No "development deal." No "demos." He handed me his number.

The next morning I called him.

"Dude, about this record deal. Were you drunk last night? If we're talking about another development deal, I have to tell you man, I'm thirty-four years old. I'm fully developed. I know what I am, who I am, what my strengths are, what my weaknesses are, and I know what I'm doing. I'm a grizzled veteran of the club circuit and I don't need nor do I want to be developed." Turns out I was preaching to the choir.

"I agree," Scott said "I just want you to do what I saw you do last night."

I was doing mostly covers, but some of them were semiobscure tunes, like Steve Cropper's "634-5789," an old R&B standard recorded by Wilson Pickett. Scott liked it so much he actually suggested we cut it, which we eventually did. I was doing it simply because it was a fun tune and a crowd-pleaser. I liked to mix in a lot of R&B and Southern rock stuff at Tillie's. I did whatever I felt like doing, even if I wasn't carrying the torch for traditional country music. I thought, "What the hell. This is what I like." You can call my music whatever you want to call it. But I never signed on to become some kind of Neo-Retro-New-Traditionalist-Hat-Guy or whatever the hell they call us singers these days. That wasn't my deal, so please, I begged Scott, don't put that label and burden on me. If you do, I'll most certainly let you down.

Now, over the years, we've seen that I'm definitely not what you'd call a traditionalist. I love country. R&B. Southern rock. Blues. Great songs and moving stories. I was writing my own songs, too, including a tune called "There's a Girl in Texas," one that Scott liked well enough to consider making it my first single. There's an old truism in Nashville that if you're good enough, eventually somebody is going to hear about you and come check you out.

While I don't like to brag, there are some people who are unbelievable singers, and they've got the chops, and the voice, but there's that other elusive "thing" that most singers don't have. You really don't know what that "thing" is until you see somebody onstage in front of a crowd who has "it." Believe me, your beer joint audience is your ultimate jaded audience. They couldn't care less who you are. In fact, they didn't even come down to hear you. They came to dance, shoot pool, drink beer, and meet the ladies, and not necessarily in that order. I just happened to be the band onstage that night. However, I guess I had that "thing," whatever it is. And that's what Scott saw. I had a rapport with the people. I could talk to them, make fun of me, make fun of them, laugh at them, and fight with them. I was one of them. I just happened to be up there singing Waylon Jennings songs while I was partying with them. We all had the same agenda: Have a good time. I think Scott saw that and knew it could translate onto a bigger stage with some record label grooming.

Sometimes making it in life comes down to sheer luck. I'm living proof that luck has a lot to do with success. There are an untold number of successful people in this world who made it out of sheer, unearned, undeserved luck, from being in the right place at the right time when something good happened.

I've been lucky all my life. When Rhonda introduced me to Scott at the baggage claim and told him where I was singing, might I have gotten a record deal anyway? What was lucky was that I had the opportunity to speak to him directly. It turns out he was so impressed with my *speaking* voice that he later told Rhonda that if I could just stay on pitch then he wanted to hear what I sounded like singing onstage. And that's why he came to hear me. He was intrigued by the timbre of my voice.

After Scott and I had been working together for a while he told me that what he thought was unique about my voice was the fact that it's a bass that "cuts" like a tenor. While bass voices are generally duller, I have a low voice with an edge to it. So when Scott *officially* became the president of Capitol Nashville, he called me right away. "You are my guy, the first act I'm signing." Like Rhonda, Scott put it all on the black for me.

Scott and I went immediately to work. Fortunately, at the time, I was working for a guy who built barns and decks. My boss also loved music and he liked me, too, so if I ever needed time off to collaborate with a writer or sing on a demo, not only did he adjust my schedule, but he encouraged me. He wanted me to make it, so he worked with me, and let me have the latitude I needed to pursue my music while at the same time letting me work hard and make some money. I appreciated him so much. As a result, when I got to the point where I bought some farmland and could afford to hire somebody to help build my own barns, I knew exactly who to call. Greg and I are still good friends to this day.

While it may have been a smart move relocating to Nashville, it was never a do-or-die thing. That's what kept me relaxed in front of a crowd when Scott first saw me, my sheer lack of desperation. Music was my dream, but if I couldn't make it, I'd survive. No big deal. Nashville was more like, I'll go up there, hang out for a while, and see how it goes. If it didn't work out, there was always the oil field. And that's really the way I felt about my music career.

I had set a goal and given myself a cutoff point. Thirty-five years of age and that's it. If I didn't have a record deal by the time I turned thirty-five, I would go back to working for the man so I could get vested enough toward some kind of retirement plan. I had a family, and I had finally matured to the point that I wasn't going to waste time chasing some stupid unattainable dream, letting my children go hungry and putting those I loved at risk.

The initial record deal process with Capitol went relatively quickly because both parties wanted it to happen. When the lawyers got involved, it seemed to drag on a bit for me because I was itching and ready to go into the studio and cut a record.

Fortunately for me, and with the help and belief of Scott and Rhonda, I got in right under the wire. I inked my deal at age thirty-four, signing the contract at the end of 1995, one year before my thirty-five-years-old deadline. By the time my first single, "There's a Girl in Texas," was scheduled to come out in 1996, I knew I had a long dusty road of more dues paying ahead of me.

Chapter Fifteen

SWING, BATTER, BATTER:
FOOTBALL VS. SOCCER, NASCAR, AND 'SHINE

'M GLAD THE WORLD CUP IN SOCCER IS ONLY HELD EVERY four years. I hate soccer, I just abhor it. I think American soccer is some kind of international conspiracy—I don't know from where it's being instigated, I suspect Europe—but it is an attempt to pussify the entire nation. I swear to God it is. The whole soccer mom phenomenon is a creation of some pacifist organization out to castrate an entire generation of sports-loving American men, and I think the sport should be abolished.

One time some moron booked me to sing after a professional (MLS) soccer game in Tampa. I didn't know we were following a game until we got there and my road manager warned me, "Don't say anything about the soccer game. They lost."

"Okay."

I went onstage and I sang a few songs, and then I said, "How did y'all's kickball game come out?"

I heard a little smattering of boos, and I went on, "Hey, I'm just kidding. You know, I like soccer, really. I think it's excellent training for future field goal kickers."

There was another small round of boos, and I let it go until the end of the show. And then I said, "Thank you for having us here at your little soccer thing. And all joking aside, I do enjoy soccer. Sissies need games to play, too."

My road manager grabbed me and said, "We'd better get out of here. You pissed these people off so bad, they don't even want to pay us. Let's just get on the bus."

"They're really that upset?"

I never performed at a soccer game after that. The next day the local paper said, "Adkins calls players sissies." That team didn't last much longer in Tampa, and I like to think maybe I had a hand in destroying it.

Soccer's status as the most popular sport in the world is no mystery to me. Soccer is king because soccer is cheap. All you need is a ball and a bunch of energetic young kids and you've got yourself a game. No bats, gloves, shoulder pads, or cleats. Just a ball and a couple of designated goals.

My favorite sport, hands down, is football. I like boxing, too, although I never get to go to any of the big fights. I'm also a big NASCAR fan because I know some of the drivers, and that makes it more fun. NASCAR is the largest spectator sport in America, and has the second-largest total TV viewership, right behind the National Football League. It's also one of our most misunderstood sports. The so-called sports experts/pundits are all over the road about it. Talk show host Jim Rome has made hillbilly references about NASCAR being just a series of endless left turns, while John Salley of *The Best Damn Sports Show Period* has defended NASCAR and admits that there is athleticism, extreme concentration, and endurance involved.

Novices look at NASCAR on television and they think, Well, how silly is that? I'll admit that NASCAR is like a lot of sports, in that television can capture only so much of the dynamics and excitement. For example, a televised NBA game might seem like a routine hoop shoot until you go see a game live. If you sit courtside directly behind the basket at an NBA game you'll see seven-foot guys swatting at each other and throwing elbows just to score two lousy points. Up close, it's a war zone down there, yet on TV it doesn't look half as brutal. Same thing when you watch the Nextel Cup on TV. You don't see the intensity, feel the danger, hear the high-decibel noise, or experience the frenzy of the pit crews.

There again, you have to understand history to really appreciate NASCAR and to know what it's all about. Stock car racing started in the 1920s and 1930s when moonshine runners, particularly in the South, developed reputations for speeding through highways and back roads seeing how fast they could get from point A to point B for their bootlegger clients. It became a competition. Pretty soon, after Prohibition was lifted in 1933, their business dried up. So they started organizing contests and competitions to see who the best drivers were.

That was the impetus for how it began. Runnin' 'shine.

I definitely think NASCAR is a sport! In this ADD world we live in today, we can't seem to be able to keep our attention focused on one thing long enough to see it through. For those guys to be able to drive 160 miles per hour for five hundred miles takes an incredible amount of focus, and it's taxing. You're never completely relaxed in that car, and it's hot as Hades in there. You don't ever get to pull over and piss. There's also a lot of strategy involved in psyching out your opponents on the track. It's a lot more involved than people realize.

Now, having said all that, I personally think the racing season is too long and there are too many races in some regions where they shouldn't have them. The sponsorship situation is just plain crazy, and so are some of the restrictions. I think the cars should be able to go as fast as they *can* go.

NASCAR is popular in red as well as blue states. They've got races in Delaware, New York, and California, and those are some of the places where maybe they shouldn't have races. Consider Infineon Raceway near the Napa Valley in northern California. They never ran 'shine through that place, and the locals look down their noses at the thousands of fans parked across from the track, flying their Confederate battle flags over their RVs. It's a social disconnect. Their cheese of choice is brie while mine is rat cheese on a Saltine. Having NASCAR in the Napa Valley is like having a cockfight in the lobby of the Ritz Carlton.

I don't really talk that much about the music business with my father, but in 2001, when NASCAR had their annual Busch Series race at Nashville Super Speedway, they did a tie-in with the release of my *Chrome* CD. They had these *Chrome 300* posters with my picture on them all over the place. Well, I've sold millions of records, I'm a member of the Grand Ole Opry, and I have a wall full of platinum and gold records, but when my old man saw a poster of his son at the NASCAR Busch Series, that's when he said, "Well, son, you've finally made it."

He literally grinned all day.

DESPITE THE FACT that it's the world's most popular sport, soccer bores the crap out of me. No slap to my worldwide friends, but your *fútbol* just doesn't cut it for me. Scoring opportunities are few and far between and they have ridiculous rules. For example, when a player outruns his coverage, as a wideout does in the NFL, he can still be called for offsides near the goal. Is David Beckham worth two hundred million bucks? And don't get me started on those bogus injuries you see on the soccer pitch. American sports fans cannot comprehend how some Italian pretty boy can be rolling around and writhing in pain like he's got two torn rotator cuffs, get carried off on a stretcher, then a few minutes later runs back in the game at full speed. What a crock! Maybe when little kids play soccer, it's funny and interesting to watch. But it's still a kid's backyard game to us "contact sport" loving Americans.

Baseball, on the other hand, is an intuitive sport that's more about finesse and hand-eye coordination. There is a beauty and an aesthetic to being able to hit, or throw, a curveball. There's something poetic about a pitcher who can throw junk, or heat, past a slugger with a perfect batting stroke, like Albert Pujols. The game of baseball ought to be perceived as a pure sport, because it's more dependent on strategy than on brute strength. Perhaps that's why hardcore baseball fans are so upset about the steroids controversy.

Football, on the other hand, is a very brutal sport and takes a huge toll on your body, so any player taking supplements to help them bulk up and be more able to withstand pain, I tend to give a pass. If (taken in moderation and under supervision, of course) it makes pro football more brutal, then I say, "Bring it on, hoss." It's a gladiator thing.

Baseball, on the other hand, is not about hitting the other guy. It's about hitting and throwing a baseball. And if Barry Bonds were a more likable person, he might not get booed so much. I've talked to a lot of players in Major League Baseball and nobody seems to like the guy. Sportswriters mostly despise him. He's brought a lot of grief on himself because of his superior attitude and the way he treats people.

However, baseball fans are unrealistic if they think they can keep the professional game as pure as was when they were eight years old. Baseball is much more money-driven than it was forty years ago, before free agency. Get used to it. Professional sports is all about the dough these days. You need a calculator to read the sports page.

PROFESSIONAL SPORTS IS a lot like the music business. Nothing is as fun when you get paid for it as it was when you used to do it for free. Once you start getting paid for it, it becomes a job and then some of the joy gets taken out of it. You lose a little of the pure fulfillment and the fix you get from enjoying music once you start doing it professionally. (I'm strictly speaking for myself here.) Don't get me wrong, I'm not complaining. I just can't enjoy music the same way as I used to.

We country singers are a competitive bunch. I go to concerts now and I'm listening much too critically. I'm singling out all the nuances and stage tricks of the show, how the band is playing, and what gear they're using. While I'm evaluating all of that, I'm not enjoying the music with the rest of the audience. Being a musician has also changed the way I listen to music at home and on the radio in my truck. It's just not the same as it used to be when I didn't do it for a living.

But back to sports. It's still a kids' game being played by grown professionals. I had my dreams of being a professional football player. I'm seriously envious of those who play games for a living in front of thousands of screaming fans. But trust me, once you turn professional, it's no longer like it was when you were a kid. When professional athletes sit at home and watch the playoffs, they're not just sitting there like you and I are, enjoying the game and riding the ebb and flow of the momentum. No, they're picking the game apart. They're analyzing all the offensive play calls and the defensive sets, and they're thinking about what players should or shouldn't be doing. It's like me at that concert. Is that why most pro athletes I meet say they'd rather be a singer like me, while I wish I was a ballplayer like them?

Chapter Sixteen

THE FIRST AMENDMENT DOESN'T PROTECT YOU FROM ME

S EVERYBODY KNOWS, FREEDOM OF SPEECH AND FREEDOM of the press go hand in hand. Yet these days, the free market and the information age dictate the climate of the news media. Today, we're in this wild world of the twenty-four-hour news cycle. When I was a kid, I watched the news for thirty minutes a day. That was it, unless you read the paper, and the *Springhill Press* only came out on Wednesdays.

Now a lot of people watch the news *all day long*. It's like background noise. They go about their daily routine, leaving the television tuned to Headline News, CNN, Fox News, or MSNBC. You don't even have to listen. You can read the crawl going across the bottom of the screen, 24/7. Going about our daily chores, we can glance up and see if anything's been blown up, or if something interesting is happening with the Hilton sisters, or if Anna Nicole Smith is still dead. The downside is that we're now programmed into a bunch of Chicken Littles. All day long we're being convinced the sky is falling. We're reminded of death and destruction every waking moment of our lives. We're inundated. We're anesthetized. It's everywhere.

Let's think for a moment about the Crusades. That was, without a doubt, one of the bloodiest chapters in human history. Now consider the likelihood that there were many people who lived their entire lives during that period without ever hearing a word about those campaigns. I'm talking about civilized communities, by that day's standards, that were completely oblivious to the fact that the rest of the world was at war. That's almost hard for us to comprehend. So you see, it's not that the world is any more violent than it used to be. It's that violence is more publicized now.

I do believe in the liberal media bias, and that a large majority of people in the media have a liberal slant. Over the last decade, few conservatives have been able to work for major media outlets without fear of ridicule. Sure, they can go to Fox News and not have to worry about being conservative and getting pummeled in the news workplace. I think that Fox News is just as conservatively biased as the others are liberally biased. That means I have to watch both Fox *and* CNN. I hear people complain, saying they aren't going to watch CNN because it's so slanted. But if your core beliefs are strong enough, can't you watch anything? Can't you read through the bullshit and take what you need to *learn* and put a block on the indoctrination? Can't you sort through the chaff and get the important stuff? The wheat. The facts.

If an uprising happens in Lebanon, I can watch that report on CNN. I'll see the rioting and explosions. I'll hear that this bunch and that bunch are at war with each other and that there's a curfew enforced, etc. Those are the facts. I may choose not to absorb the slant attached to the story. Instead, I just want to know what's happening.

If I could, I would watch Al Jazeera even though they're *perhaps* slanted and *possibly* biased, simply because they're going to show me pictures I'm not going to see over here. Various sources will provide you with a few more facts and more information. Then you decide. As a result, I feel like I know the score; I know what's happening and what's going on. I take advantage of the information age, so I can sort through it all and make an informed decision.

The First Amendment, I believe, is a protection that most people don't understand on a fundamental level. Or maybe it's just me, and I don't get it. The First Amendment, I thought, was designed to protect us from the government. Our founding fathers didn't want a government that the people couldn't criticize. They knew that Americans needed to be free to express themselves and criticize their government if they wanted or needed to. Not in a treasonous or traitorous way, but to criticize without fear of retaliation or repercussion. Theoretically, you can now criticize the government without fear of them breaking down your door and hauling you off to jail. At least that was the original intent.

We've now taken the First Amendment many, many steps too far by interpreting it as giving us the right to walk around and say anything we want to say without repercussion from *anybody*. People think they have the freedom to be rude, obnoxious, loud, stupid, and completely dishonest. Those are not inalienable rights afforded to you by the First Amendment, asshole. Ever hear somebody say something stupid, then dismiss it with the comment, "It's a free country, isn't it?"

In the beginning, our founding fathers were genteel. They were respectful. Well mannered. Gentlemen, by their day's standards. They didn't design the First Amendment so that everybody could be a smart-ass, shooting off their mouths and saying anything they wanted to. But that's how people interpret the First Amendment today: that they can say whatever they want, get in my face, and I can't do anything about it.

As a roughneck American, I can exercise the right not only to disagree with you, but to disagree with you violently if I choose to pay the price. That's my choice. If I choose to "disagree with you" on a physical level after you've purposely offended me, I'll deal with the consequences.

So fair warning: The First Amendment doesn't protect you from me. You might choke on your own porcelain caps if you go past the point of common courtesy and decency with me. If you insist on continuing to offend me purposefully, what little tolerance I have will disappear completely. Sorry 'bout that.

Chapter Seventeen

RIDIN' FOR THE BRAND

IGHT AFTER I SIGNED MY RECORD DEAL WITH CAPITOL,
I got a bus and hit the road. I toured in 1996 as a rookie
country recording artist. I played every free radio show from
Tallahassee to Tacoma just to get my name out there so the people
could see me, hear me, and learn a little about where I stand.

We crammed as much gear (and bodies) into that bus as we
could, and eventually we added a sixteen-foot trailer that we
dragged for half a million miles. That's equal to twenty-one times
around the globe. Then we picked up a second bus and that
worked out well for a few more years. Every step forward I took,
things got better.

I always carried a full band with at least six guys right from the
start. I was making very little money and the band needed to get
paid, so the label supported me for a while until I could increase
my market value. In the early going, you have barely enough cash
to pay for the bus, let alone cover the other expenses of touring
and playing the freebie shows. During the early phase, the label
pays for the ride because record companies know that when they
push out a new artist, they're going to have to sustain them for a
certain period of time until things catch on. Record label executives are professional gamblers. Today, things are tighter in secur-

ing label tour support. They can't spend money like they used to because of how the music industry has evolved technologically and how badly hurt their sales have been over the past seven or eight years. They just don't have the money they used to have. The late Mister Rogers might have said, "Can you say 'illegal downloads,' boys and girls?"

My first single, "There's a Girl in Texas," released in 1996, peaked at about eighteen on the charts, which was respectable, but certainly nothing to get too excited about. Luckily, the second single, "Every Light in the House Is On," went to number three. It was a classic country hurtin' tune, and it's become somewhat of a ministandard for me. I can honestly say that when I do that song at shows today, people respond to it as if it's brand-new. They sing every word at the top of their lungs, and I hope Kent's somewhere smiling. Kent Robbins, who penned hits for the Judds, George Strait, and Charley Pride, wrote that tune. A year after it became a hit, Kent died. The songwriting community lost a great one.

"(This Ain't) No Thinkin' Thing" became my first number one record. Hallelujah! Then Capitol put out a *fourth* single, "I Left Something Turned On at Home," which became my second number one. With three top fives out of the chute, I started strong.

On the strength of those four singles, my debut album, *Dreamin' Out Loud*, sold over a million copies. I thought, Man, this is going to be easy. This business is a breeze. Selling a million discs puts money in the pipeline, and while you don't see it immediately, it's comforting to know it's out there.

Then the second album, *Big Time*, came out. We released our first single, "The Rest of Mine," which went to number two. I wrote it with Kenny Beard and it was inspired by a line in the movie *Phenomenon*, starring John Travolta. There's a scene where

Travolta's character is lying in bed and he knows he's about to die, so he tells his girl that all he wants her to do is love him for the rest of his life. She looks at him and says, "No, I'm gonna love you for the rest of *mine*." I was sitting there with Kenny watching that movie and I immediately said, "There's a country song." In just a few days we had a verse and a chorus. Two weeks later we still had a verse and a chorus. We figured that was enough.

Then after "The Rest of Mine" was released my world came crashing down . . . again. The cause? Record company politics.

I was at Foxwoods Resort and Casino in Ledyard, Connecticut, in 1997 when I got a phone call telling me that my mentor, Scott Hendricks, had just been fired as president. The timing was bizarre. I had started having success, and then Deana Carter, another protégé of Scott's, came out with her first album and sold four million records! The first two projects that Scott quarterbacked had sold single and quadruple platinum. Then he got fired. What the hell? Speculation ran rampant that Garth Brooks had gotten him sacked. At the time, a lot of people thought Garth's dream was to sell more records than the Beatles. The timing couldn't have been worse for me and for everybody else on the Capitol artist roster. In my opinion, Scott wasn't fired because he was unsuccessful; it was because he wasn't doing the Garth Brooks kiss-ass dance.

After Scott got canned, they brought in a marketing guy from New York named Pat Quigley, and it seemed to me that his job was to come to Nashville and ratchet Garth Brooks's sales up to the hundred million mark. Whatever else was going on at the label with the other acts, be damned. Today all of those artists who were on Capitol Records are gone. Even Garth Brooks! Some were dropped, some asked to be let go.

But not me. I am the last man standing. I'm still at Capitol Nashville. But it came at the cost of a career slump that lasted a few years.

As a result of hanging in there, I experienced four down years that nearly broke my spirit and ruined my livelihood. My second album went gold on the strength of "The Rest of Mine." The third album, *More*, sold 250,000. I slid from a million to half a million, to a quarter-million units sold. I only had to do the math to see where the next record was headed: 125,000? Or less?

Musically and spiritually, I disassociated myself from the record label. At the first meeting I had with the new boss, FU's were quickly exchanged, and that was pretty much it for me. I did my best in the studio, but I let the label pick the singles. I was dejected, so I hit the road hard doing my county fair thing, ridin' the corndog circuit. But I was a survivor. I thought, damn, if only I can get through this regime somehow. Meanwhile, I was medicating myself, sinking further into a depression and drinking myself numb.

Up to that point, I had been doing really well. I got my deal in 1995. The hit singles started pouring out in 1996. I was doing shows straight as an arrow. I rarely had anything to drink before a show. But then it got to where I didn't much care anymore. My mood had darkened. Things were going to hell in a handbasket, and I couldn't see it getting any better. So I started drinking a little more. Then a *lot* more.

Suddenly the clouds parted and a patch of blue sky peeked through.

In 2000, Garth finally hit his coveted hundred million mark. Then Quigley split as president of Capitol Nashville and Mike Dungan came in as the new president. The sun came out again. I knew Mike when he was a vice president at Arista Nashville back when I had my development deal. I had history with Mike. He used to come out to Tillie's to hang out, drink beer, shoot pool, and listen to me sing. Not because he had to, but because I think he liked the joint. We knew each other as friends. So when he came in as the new president, I felt as if I had a new lease on life. Things were looking up and I felt a little better.

Through all the dark clouds and stormy times, I never let the quality of my work suffer. I almost always went into the studio sober, because when I didn't the recording was unusable. To this day, I vehemently stand behind my third album, *More,* because it's a damn fine CD. Trey Bruce produced it beautifully, and it still holds up today when you compare it against anything I've ever done. Sure, they might have picked all the wrong singles and the album didn't get promoted properly and it didn't get a fair shake, but that doesn't tarnish the quality of the music. Once Mike came in, my next CD, *Chrome,* was an album that was a stylistic change for me. The title track was something fresh and different—my own brand of pop, rappin', crunk, country . . . aw hell. I don't know what it is.

Looking back, I'm glad I stuck with Capitol Records and that I kept ridin' for the brand. To this day, in light of the drinking and the darkness, I still don't know why I didn't hang up my spurs and split. Although I thought about quitting, there was something inside telling me that if I could only stick it out, things would be all right on the other side of the storm.

But while my career was back on course, my drinking had gotten out of control. People around me had become concerned. I was in denial and soon I would learn, the hard way, that I needed to stop.

Chapter Eighteen

DIFFERENT KINDS OF BOTTOMS

. . .

ALL I CAN DO IS ALL I CAN DO
AND I KEEP ON TRYIN'.

—"I'm Tryin'"
from *Chrome*

OMETIMES THE HIGH TIMES ARE NOT ALL THEY SEEM. I remember when I, thankfully, got my first number one country record, "(This Ain't) No Thinkin' Thing," from my debut album, *Dreamin' Out Loud*. It hit the top spot in 1996. I was playing a dinky casino in Michigan out in the middle of nowhere. It was snowing outside and my band and I were getting ready for the show when we heard the news. The casino lounge I was playing at held around 250 people. I walked out on the stage that night and made my proud announcement: "Well, it's a big day for me. I have the number one song in country music."

"Yeah, sure you do," the audience seemed to react. Tough crowd. Not quite the reaction I had pictured in my dreams. Yet there we were in Michigan for three whole days, snowbound, playing two shows a night with the number one song in country.

Welcome to the big time!

By the time I began work on my fourth record, *Chrome*, in 2001, I was still backsliding but recovering from the damage inflicted during the previous Capitol regime. Mike Dungan, Capitol's new president, was determined to help me regain my platinum status. I had some solid material lined up for the new record. Songwriters Jeffrey Steele and Anthony Smith wrote two killer tunes, one being the title track, "Chrome," and a ballad (co-written with Chris Wallin) called "I'm Tryin'." That song is especially personal and signifies the ups and downs of my career. As the song says, I had been constantly climbing—and falling off—the mountain of success.

"I'm Tryin'" deals with the human struggle and the reality of our day-to-day existence. As long as you try, it's the best you can do. We're never going to meet everybody's expectations, but once you stop tryin', you're worthless. The song is about a man who falls short all the time and disappoints people regularly. He's trying to tell folks he doesn't fall short on purpose. "I don't disappoint on purpose. Really, I don't. I'm trying. I'm doing the best I can here."

By the summer of 2001, I had all my ducks lined up. My record label was firmly back in my corner. Then I had *another* setback, but this time I had nobody to blame but myself.

On July 5, 2001, I was pulled over on suspicion of driving under the influence. It made the news and word spread like wildfire all over Nashville (as if nobody in that town ever drinks too much). I decided it was best to be straight up about it. When I got the charge, I just owned up. I didn't go through the bullshit that some famous people do, which is to hire a highfalutin lawyer, piss and moan, and drag it through court for a long time until a conviction melts down to a slap on the wrist or case dismissed.

I figured the judge would throw the book at my ass anyway. They could have easily made an example of me. "Entertainer drives drunk!" Since I decided to own up, I knew I was going to get convicted and that I was not going to get off.

Besides, the cops had videotape of me doing stupid human tricks and not performing them very well. And cussing? Ooooeeee. I cussed like a sailor. I cussed the cop, the city, the county, the world, the whole nine yards. I was shit-the-bed drunk that July night.

In my case, the wheels of justice ground slowly on their own. I didn't appear in court until November, a full four months after the deed was done. On that day I went to court basically to fess up. I admitted I was guilty and said I was sorry. I shouldn't have driven under the influence and sworn at the police. That day I was sitting on a bench out in the hall, close to a holding room filled with state troopers, I suppose all appearing in court on their own cases. One of the state troopers popped his head out of the room and asked me, "Mr. Adkins, could you please step in here for a minute?"

Damn. I walked into the holding room fully expecting all those cops to chew my ass out for going off on one of their own.

"We just wanted to tell you, on behalf of the state troopers of the state of Tennessee, we appreciate your attitude during this whole ordeal, and that you've owned up to what you did. You admitted you made a mistake. You didn't go through the whole blame game scenario, and you didn't try to weasel out." That meant a lot to me.

Now . . . community service? No thanks. I never understood those people who opt to go out on Saturday morning and pick up trash. I said to myself, "I ain't doin' it." So I asked, respectfully, how long I would have to spend in jail?

"Forty-eight hours."

Hell, that's nothing, I said to myself. I can do forty-eight hours standing on my head in three feet of manure.

So after sentencing I went down to the Williamson County Jail and did my two days. Jail didn't scare me much. I'm a big boy and can take care of myself. The correctional officers (COs) at the jail decided against putting me in with the general population. So they ordered me to stay with the trusties, which was cool of them to do. They were the clerks who ran the place and the janitors who mopped the floors and swept up. They had been there for a while and gained some seniority. I had no say in the matter and they didn't have to do it. That was the only break they cut me. I did the crime and I did the time.

Once a correctional officer woke me up in my cell at three o'clock in the morning.

"Hey man, get up."

"What's up?"

"I need you to sign this." The CO asked me to sign a few autographs for him. What else was I gonna do?

A few years later my wife and I went to the Cadillac dealership to buy a carbon-emitting, ozone-destroying, luxurious Escalade (which we love, by the way). While we were standing out front, I heard this guy call out to me, "Hey Trace."

I looked over and there was this black dude in the flower bed planting shrubs. "Remember me?" he asked.

"I'm sorry, I don't."

"Me and you! We were in the same cell together in the county jail."

"Oh yeah, man! How's it going?" There I was, standing in the shrubs shaking hands and having a chat with my ex-cellmate while my wife was desperately trying to distract the salesman. I looked over in time to see her "flash" the poor man! A little over the top, I thought.

AFTER I DID my two days, I didn't run and hide in rehab. In fact, it was over a year after I went to county jail that I finally went into alcohol rehab. My DUI conviction was only one of many signals that my drinking had gotten out of control. There wasn't one single event or a major catastrophe that precipitated my going into rehab. Jail was only one signpost on the way. But it had gotten to the point where my drinking was getting potentially deadly. Worse, I was isolating myself from my loved ones.

Once I got pulled over, I knew I couldn't drink in a town where people could regularly see me. Back then I was a pretty mean drunk. Not just a mean drunk—I was the drunk in charge. When I got hammered, I was in charge of whatever environment and situation I was in. Whenever I was drunk, I was a walking ugly scene in the making and I knew it. An addict is that way. However, nobody feels as guilty about the things they do when they're under the influence as the person who does them once he sobers up. I think of the guilt that I'll carry all the time for the people I have offended or made angry or whose feelings I have hurt while I was on a drunk. Believe me, that's a heavy burden to bear.

In 2002 I started taking extreme measures to, I thought, protect myself. I headed out to my farm, locked the gate, went out to the barn, and polluted myself. I would stay there for two or three days at a time and at the rate I was drinking, somebody was going to go out there one day and find me dead. A disagreement with a Kawasaki Mule almost brought that to pass.

One day during this period I was on the side of a hill behind the barn driving a farm utility vehicle. A Kawasaki Mule is basically a four-wheel-drive, heavy-duty golf cart with a steel roll cage. The roll cage will save you from serious injury in the event of a rollover, provided you are using the seat belt. I, of course, was not.

To make an admission of incredible stupidity a little less humiliating, I'll cut to the chase. I ended up lying on my back in some rocks with the Mule lying on its side on top of me. The only parts of my body sticking out were my head (thank God) and my right arm. Not panicking, because I was most certainly hammered, I noticed the antenna of my cell phone hanging out of the bib pocket of my overalls and grabbed it with my free hand. Now . . . "Who are you gonna call, dumbass?" Luckily, my friend Bobby, who lives about a mile down the road and, most important, owns a backhoe and a key to my place, answered the phone and hurried on over. I only had to stay in the hospital for a couple of days that time.

The bottom line is this: I'm an alcoholic, and alcoholics don't need a logical reason to drink themselves into trouble. If it's raining, then let's have a drink because it is a gloomy day. If it's sunny outside, then let's celebrate because it is a beautiful day.

In a way, I do buy into the whole alcoholism-is-a-disease thing. Alcoholism is a strange phenomenon. They say it's a progressive disease in the sense that it will keep progressing whether you're drinking or not. In other words, as the years go by, whether you drink or not, if you're not dealing with solving your drinking problem, your alcoholism is still going to continue to get worse. I also knew I couldn't go back to drinking socially and just have a pop or two. In my case, if I fell off the wagon, I was going to be a lush. I needed to confront my demons posthaste. Whether any of this twelve-step stuff was 100 percent true, who knew? All I know is that it took a full-scale intervention to get me to stop boozing.

The first time I was confronted about my drinking was back in

1987 by the guys in Bayou, when I was twenty-five years old and playing all those beer joints. Back then I was young and immortal. Stupid and bullheaded. My logic: "I'm supposed to be drunk, ain't I? Hell, we're playing beer joints and honky-tonks every night. What do you expect?"

It was quite a different scene in 2002, when my wife and my manager, aided by a trained professional, intervened. Using a professional is definitely the best way to stage an intervention. Your family and loved ones shouldn't stage it on their own. You need someone who knows the ropes—somebody who's been through it, who has enough understanding and skill to handle a heavy confrontational experience. He or she might have a few letters and degrees after their name, though they're not necessarily a psychiatrist or psychologist or anything like that.

My intervention was like an ambush. Everybody in the room had letters they had written. And worse, they waited for the exact right moment before they sat me down, a day after I'd gotten really shitfaced and woken up feeling like crap, all hungover. That's when they pounced, right after I'd already beaten myself up pretty bad with the booze. As they pummeled me with words and feelings, I was really on the spot. This time I really heard what everyone had to say, and this time I decided they were right. It was time to own up to my drinking problem once and for all.

So on December 17, 2002, they threw my sorry ass into detox and for the first three or four days, I was pissed. I wasn't mad at the people who sent me there, the interventionists, I was angry at myself for how I had ended up: institutionalized.

They kept me on Valium for three or four days so I wouldn't leave. They gradually weaned me off the Valium and I started going to meetings. Lots of meetings! Every day. Get up at the crack of dawn, go to a meeting. Eat breakfast, go to another meeting. Lunch, meeting. It was nonstop interaction.

At first my goal was to go through the whole twelve-step thing, but I soon realized that I was not twelve-step material. I took a different approach, a more pragmatic angle. I just wanted to quit drinking, not replace alcohol with a new religion. That's not, in any way, a slight against people who depend on Alcoholics Anonymous to stay sober. More power to you.

Because I didn't graduate through all the steps, real hardcore twelve-step people might consider me a relapse waiting to happen. Step One: I admit I'm powerless over alcohol and that my life has become unmanageable. In my opinion, once you get past that big one, the jig is up. So I surrendered.

What really happened to me was that about twenty-one days into rehab, I was finally clearheaded, for the first time in years. I had plenty of time on my hands to think things through, and I had an epiphany. I had a "direct moment of clarity" where I said to God and myself, "Lord, look at me. I've got the world by the cojones, and all I have to do is keep my act together for another decade or so, and I can retire. I may never have to work again! I mean *really* work! Again! Ever!"

And that's how you win at the game of life. You count your blessings, honestly assess your talents and skills, and move on. No blame game. No pity party. In the poker game of life, I've been dealt at least a full house, maybe even four of a kind. Some of those poor bastards I was befriended by in there weren't holding any cards at all. They had lost their jobs, their families, their friends, and their self-respect. Rock bottom.

That's something else I learned. Everybody's "bottom" is different. (No, not that bottom, you pervert.) You can stop the downward spiral anytime you choose to, and keep your bottom from being one where you're lying in the gutter. I recognized that I was headed in that direction and was given the chance to stop the skid. My bottom was a high bottom. The very best kind, if you know what I mean. (Okay, I'm a pervert, too.)

That's how I look at rehab, and what it did for me. If I can just keep my shit together a little while longer and make some damned good music, I can beat the system. I can win. That's the way I've been going at it ever since.

I've been through some heavy times, just like everybody else. Divorces are certainly painful, but the most pain I was ever in was when I lost my baby brother Scott to a car crash in 1993. He was a great kid. He was just twenty-one when he got killed and it was terrible, the most excruciating moment of my life. I loved that kid, he loved me, and I think of him every day.

Scott never lived to see my success, and that's a shame since he was my biggest fan. I had only moved to Nashville the year before and nothing had really happened, yet. During the summer between his junior and senior year of high school, I took him out on the road with me for a couple of months of honky-tonkin' and partying. He thought I was a star *then*. We had a blast. We were true buddies. We fished and hunted and did a lot of things brothers often do together.

Scott wanted to be like me, so maybe, I think, I corrupted the poor kid. I've had to deal with that issue ever since. In some ways I feel responsible. He always wanted to be like me. Was it ultimately my fault, him wanting to be like me, getting drunk and dying so young?

His death devastated my parents. As a result, my brother and I pretty much had to take care of everything and make all the arrangements. Understandably, my parents were basket cases, but it was really hard for me, too. It was the first time I'd ever seen my father shed one single tear. So when I pulled up to the house and my daddy came walking out to my truck, I knew things were bad. I saw him age ten years over the next 365 days. His heart was broken. As he cried on my shoulder, I ended up having to be the strong one. My mother was on another planet. Planet Grief.

Scott and my daddy were super tight. My father certainly did a fine job raising me and my younger brother Clay, but by the time my baby brother came along, he had matured to a point in his life where he knew exactly what being a father was all about. He knew how to nurture Scott, and at the same time make him act right. They were really close friends. He was Ward Cleaver to my baby brother, and they talked about everything.

I may get crucified by all those experts who write those self-help books for saying this, but I don't equate love with constant communication. When I was a teenager, my daddy and I would go weeks without speaking, while living in the same house. There wasn't anything wrong. There were no problems. Everything was cool. There was unspoken communication between us. We didn't have to talk. I did my job around the house being a good kid. He did his, being a good dad.

So what did we have to talk about?

Even now, I'll go weeks before I talk to my father. I love him to death, and God knows we're tighter now than ever, but I've never been about being in constant communication, and my wife can't wrap her head around it because she's the exact opposite. Rhonda sometimes speaks to her family several times a day.

I sang at my brother's funeral. It was the toughest gig I have ever done but I knew he would have wanted me to, so I had to "cowboy up" and do it. After I sang I read a poem . . . something about his now being numbered among the angels.

There's a song I later recorded on my second album called "Out of My Dreams." It reminded me of my baby brother, so I recorded it for him. On the surface, it may sound like a love song, but I know the guy who co-wrote it, Doug Nichols, and the first time he saw me sing it live, he was standing on the side of the stage. As I came off the stage, he walked up to me.

"You sing that song for your brother, don't you?"

I swallowed hard. "Yes I do."

"Well, I wrote that song for *my* brother." Doug's brother had also been killed.

All sorts of thoughts flow through my brain whenever I sing that song. And Scott shows up some nights in my dreams and it's like he never left. In my dreams, we spend a whole day together. Every time I sing that song, I want to see Scott, hug him, and tell him that I miss him and love him.

It's all I can do. And I'm tryin'.

Chapter Nineteen

RUN FOR THE BORDER

LLEGAL IMMIGRATION IS DEFINITELY AN ISSUE WHERE BIG money gets the votes in Congress. Contrary to what some folks may say, it's not about race. Polls show that *all* ethnic groups favor lowering legal immigration quotas as well as enforcing existing laws against illegal immigration. While the politicians talk about justice and opportunity, they're simultaneously selling amnesty to the cheap labor lobbies and huge corporations and looking for cheap votes from ethnic political machines. Corporations and ethnic activists . . . strange bedfellows indeed! Doesn't anybody realize that the people hardest hit by illegal immigration are the working poor—black, white, Asian, and Hispanic—segment of the labor force?

As a result, honest working-class occupations like meatpacking, unskilled construction work, and a whole lot of other entry-level jobs that used to pay decent wages don't anymore. Turn on the cheap labor spigot and you've got a self-fulfilling prophecy: They've suddenly become "jobs Americans won't do." People ask, "Who'll pick the crops?" That's not really the question. The real question is, "Who'll pick the crops cheaper than anybody else?"

Our country's immigration heritage is important. But immigration today, legal and illegal, is out of control, running at five and six times the normal flow rate. If we go back to the level of legal immigration we had before 1965 and simply start enforcing the laws against illegal immigration, we'll still be the most open society in the world by far. Immigration enforcement would not only level the playing field for skilled workers and apprentices but would give wages a chance to catch up with inflation. The working man and woman have seen their paychecks stagnate in real dollars since the 1970s, when Congress initiated big legal immigration increases and encouraged illegal immigration by dangling amnesty programs.

Looking back, there was never supposed to be such big increases in legal immigration. When Senator Edward Kennedy and his cronies pushed the 1965 Hart-Celler Act abolishing national origin quotas through Congress (and later the 1990 Immigration Act), they promised that immigration numbers would not go up for more than a couple of years. Instead, the numbers have consistently gone up to more than a million people a year legally and more than half a million a year illegally. That put the number of estimated illegals in this country at twelve million.

The illegal immigration controversy has cut across party lines. The Republicans had total control of every branch of government and still didn't do a damn thing about it. So now it's their fault. But mainly it all comes down to a lack of leadership. If only somebody from government and industry would stand up and be straight up with the American people and tell us the consequences, like orange juice is going to cost an extra quarter a gallon; tomatoes and lettuce will be a little more expensive. If the lawmakers would just straight-out tell us the economic result of tightening immigration law enforcement, we could ponder the information, be better informed, and be a lot less likely to bitch and complain.

I'm not saying we need to round people up and deport them,

although the legislation that would require illegal aliens to process their citizenship by first returning to their native lands and reentering legally sounds like a good idea. We don't have to be in any way inhumane. Nor do we need to pass a bunch of new laws. The laws on the books are good ones, with plenty of protection for bona fide refugees and individual rights.

As far as our borders, the onus cannot be on the Mexicans to tighten up their border. It's on us to protect our own borders. As long as billions of dollars are rolling into Mexico from our economy, it's a great deal for Mexico. That's why Mexican agencies pass out pamphlets and travel brochures instructing people on how to cross the border, where to go when you get across, and how to function once you get here.

HERE'S A PARABLE for you. Say Redneck Bubba lives in the trailer park across town. He doesn't like living in the trailer park. The pool is scummy. His neighbors' dogs piss in his flower bed. The other kids are beating his kids up. It's total mayhem in the trailer park. So Bubba decides he's gonna hook his trailer up to his pickup truck and drive down to the nice gated community where they frequently forget to keep the gate closed.

In goes Bubba. He finds an open spot of ground somewhere and parks his trailer. Presto! Bubba now lives in the nice gated community with the tennis courts, the golf course, and a nice pool minus the scum. Plus, Bubba's delighted to live under the protection of the security guards who are supposed to be watching the gate. Pretty soon he's got cars sitting up on blocks in the yard that he hasn't mowed in six months. His naked kids are running wild all around the neighborhood terrorizing the neighborhood soccer team.

Bubba didn't actually buy the property, nor is he paying his monthly upkeep dues and fees. Yet there Bubba lives in a beautiful and exclusive community going on four or five years. Make no mistake. Everybody else is pissed off about it. They paid a lot of money to live in the nice neighborhood and they're bitching and raising hell to the property management company, who do nothing, even though Bubba's breaking the law. You see, some of the nearby residents pay Bubba on the cheap to keep up their yards instead of hiring the gardeners who work hard doing business on the up-and-up. Still, legally, nobody is forcing Bubba to leave. Then one day Bubba pays a fine. Now it seems he can stay indefinitely with his trailer.

I know, it's a ridiculous scenario. It could never happen here. Or could it? That's why the American public screams at Congress about immigration amnesty. We pay a lot of taxes and spend a lot of money in order to live in this exclusive community we call the United States of America, where we enjoy all kinds of beautiful benefits. We know that America is a magnet that draws people from all over the world. But sorry, if you can't pay the monthly dues and go through the proper channels of arrival, you shouldn't be able to stay. And that's why Bubba needs to hook up his trailer and get the hell out! Sorry, Bubba, nothing personal. It's got nothing to do with your pickup truck or your cowboy hat. The bottom line is that the lucky citizens of the United States of America have paid sweat equity to live here only to watch it become culturally destroyed.

In other words, what if the people inside the gated community suddenly threw the gates open and shouted out, "Hey! Everybody come on in and enjoy our pool, our golf course, and our tennis courts!" How long would it be before there was scum in the pool and the golf course was all chewed up after Bubba's been out there spinning doughnuts on the green in his four-wheel-drive, and throwing his beer cans out the window? No one would tolerate that because it isn't fair. Yet, as a country, we tolerate a similar sad scenario. The U.S.A. is a big, huge gated community, built and maintained by the citizens, and that's why we simply can't just throw the gate open and let everybody in. At its core, it's not fair.

Some things in life involve the luck of the draw. I wasn't born in Mexico. I wasn't born in Nicaragua. I wasn't born in Afghanistan. But that's not my fault. By the luck of the draw, I was born in a small town in Louisiana. Just because your lot in life isn't as good as mine doesn't make it my fault or responsibility.

This brings us back to the issue of guilt. We have and enjoy the freedoms and perks of this beautiful country because we have fought and worked hard to create them. Should we feel guilty that the rest of the world isn't like us? What we gladly offer to them is a page out of our playbook, and lots of countries are taking advantage of it. Day by day, countries in Asia, Africa, South America, and Europe are becoming more and more Americanized and modern through their own hard work ethic and emphasis on education. Do what we've done and create your own gated community. We'll gladly help you because we're not selfish or unwilling to share our knowledge. On the contrary. Here's our Constitution. Here's how we did it. You can do it in your country, too.

SOMETIMES IT'S DIFFICULT to figure out which side our government is on. Take the case of Jose Alonso Compean and Ignacio Ramos, two U.S. Border Patrol agents sentenced in October 2006 to eleven- and twelve-year prison terms for shooting a drug-smuggling suspect in the gluteus maximus as he fled across the United States–Mexico border.

After a two-week trial, a federal jury convicted them of causing serious bodily injury, assault with a deadly weapon, discharge of a firearm in relation to a crime of violence, *and* a civil rights violation.

According to the assistant U.S. attorney who prosecuted the case on behalf of the smuggler's civil rights, "agents are not allowed to pursue. In order to exceed the speed limit, you have to get supervisor approval, and they did not."

It was only after the fact, after the suspect's mother called federal authorities in El Paso from Mexico complaining that her son was shot in the ass fleeing Border Patrol agents, that our own government chose not only to proactively prosecute the case, but in order to sweeten the pot since the suspect was reticent to testify, they awarded the alleged suspect complete *immunity* for trying to haul almost eight hundred pounds of pot into the United States. On top of that, American taxpayers footed the bill for the suspect's quality American medical care.

I can only assume that whenever our agents choose to play hardball with illegal immigrant drug smugglers, instead of enforcing the law, our federal government sends the wrong message that says it's okay for criminals to run back across the border for safety, even after abandoning a van full of drugs, in this case 743 pounds of marijuana. By the way, Ramos took a sound beating inside prison walls by a group of Mexican gangsters. The convicted agents' requests to be released on bond pending appeal have been rejected.

I say if President George Bush (or whoever) doesn't pardon Agents Ramos and Compean, then he (or she) doesn't have a hair on their ass.

I BELIEVE THE easiest way to solve the illegal immigration enforcement problem is to go after the employers who hire illegal aliens. When we knowingly employ people who are illegal in this country, we all should be held accountable and pay dearly. There are a lot of large companies who secretly want our borders to remain as porous as they are, though they'll never admit to it. There are companies in all kinds of industries that base their entire business model and profit return on hiring illegal immigrants. If we crack down on the minority of bad corporate citizens, then the majority of good corporate citizens can compete on a fairer playing field. After we seal the borders, attrition will shrink the illegal immigration dilemma.

After years of neglect, this isn't a problem that's going to be easily rectified in a matter of a few years. Once you seal the border, the remedy of enforcement is going to take time. If the federal and state politicians won't do it, then local people are going to take justice into their own hands and deal with it. This whole fence idea is a good idea, but it's going to take forever to build.

A push toward immigration enforcement is a trend that is coming to your town. And you'll be seeing more and more communities taking sides on the immigration debate. You'll see safe havens being set up as well as towns passing ordinances and making statements against hiring illegal workers. That is what Clarksville, Tennessee, did: If you are a landlord and you rent to illegals and you know it, then you're going to get fined and go to jail.

It's not just the corporations, special interests, lobbyists, and politicians who are the culprits. It comes down to you and me on a personal level. We have to make a personal choice, whether we want to do what's right or what's cheaper. Ultimately we're paying a huge price for cheaper nannies for kids, cheaper lawn care, or cheaper whatever.

I was guilty of it. There was a day when I used to gladly do my own yard work all the time, but since my life has gotten so insane,

I can't do it anymore. So my wife hired a landscaping company to take care of our yard. I never paid much attention to the gardeners in the yard. They worked hard and did a great job.

Eventually, this issue really started rearing up, and I thought, you know, the problem is that people like me are perpetuating this thing by turning a blind eye to it. I for one am not going to do that anymore. So I called the guy who ran the landscaping company and I told him, "Look, don't send anybody to work on my property if they don't have green cards and proper documentation. There will be nobody working in my yard without proper documentation. And if I go out and stop one of these guys on the mower and he doesn't have it, then I'm gonna politely send him out of my yard and confiscate the mower. Then, when you come to get the mower, we'll call the cops, the Department of Homeland Security, and Immigration and Customs Enforcement and we'll talk about which laws have been broken and whether you get your mower back." That rectified the situation. I remain vigilant.

There was another example that came about on the home front. Recently my wife and I were talking to a contractor about building a house for our family, and he wanted to take us over to another place he was building in order to show us his workmanship and crew.

We got to the job site and there looked to be undocumented workers all over the place. I looked at him and said, "I know some of these guys are probably illegal workers. They're not gonna build my house, are they?"

The contractor looked at me as if to say, "I don't know how we can build your house without illegal workers." That was the last time I spoke to the guy. I guess we've now become so addicted to cheap labor that legitimate American craftsmen are being lowballed out of honest work.

You can't be complacent or apathetic and act like immigration enforcement isn't your problem and that you can't do anything about it. Everybody in this country has to decide to play an active role instead of being passive about it and pointing the finger at everybody else and waiting for "the man" to enforce the law. Take a stand and say, "I'm not gonna participate in this, and I'm not gonna be a part of this problem."

If everybody had that attitude, the problem would go away. This isn't about being racist. It's about charity and justice beginning at home and paying a decent wage to poor American workers, black, white, and Hispanic. I'm willing to pay more to have good ol' American boys of all races and legal immigrants build my house. Give me the figure if you use legal workers, give me the figure if you use illegal workers and I'll meet you part way. We'll haggle, and eventually agree on a fair price that lets me look my neighbors in the eye with a clear conscience.

Chapter Twenty

THE LUCKY 12,000,000+

I'T'S BEEN SAID A MILLION TIMES THAT WE ARE A COUNTRY of immigrants. The truth is we are a planet of immigrants, except for some dude that lives in the center of Africa where scientists claim humankind started. A century ago, some of us came on ships and were processed through Ellis Island, where there was a record of our arrival. We were tagged, counted, renamed, categorized, and accounted for.

Before that, the immigrants who originally founded this country set up a charter as to how we were going to run things. After stealing the land from the native inhabitants, they set up their own form of government, made their own rules, and eventually created the Constitution. Now we live by those original laws. It's how we conduct ourselves. That means subsequent immigrants can't just come in here and break or change the rules set up by the original immigrants. Nor, on the other hand, can I move to another country and change *their* rules to reflect my values. No other country would allow me to do that.

I can't understand the people who insist there's nothing we can do about the 12,000,000+ illegals already in this country. Shrugging our shoulders in resignation is like saying that since St. Jude's Hospital hasn't found a cure for cancer we should quit trying. Ignoring the problem in hopes that it'll go away or just giving up is not the answer.

Loading people up on buses and deporting them isn't the answer, either. Not only is it inhumane and impossible, there's a better way. You don't have to scour the country looking for and rounding up illegals. I remember when I had outstanding speeding tickets I hadn't paid (because I didn't have any money), so there was a bench warrant out for my arrest. The cops didn't have to come looking for me. Instead, they patiently waited until the next time they caught me speeding, and then they took me off to jail. People surface and pop up. And when they do, if someone's not here legally, they're on the next train or bus to the border, on their way home.

The argument that we can't deal with the 12,000,000+ people here illegally is ludicrous. They didn't come here in ninety days, and we aren't going to process them in ninety days. It will take as long to eradicate the problem as it took for the problem to take root. Processing 12,000,000+ sounds like enough of a daunting task when you consider the fact that the average working stiff can't even get his or her driver's license renewed without standing in a line all day long.

Illegals have been breaking the law in our country for as many years as they've been in this country. They've made X amount of dollars, some of it tax-free, not to mention burdening our infrastructure. So if we just let them come in and apply for a "Z visa" and pay a fine and say all is forgiven and forgotten, I say why can't we do that for every other lawbreaker? If this is their deal, where, as an American citizen, can I sign up for amnesty? What about the guy who's wanted for tax evasion, or more serious violent crimes like drug dealing, rape, and murder? All he has to do is surrender, pay five thousand dollars, and he gets a secured identification and we let him go?

Some call it a penalty, not amnesty. Let me tell you, if I hadn't paid taxes for the past five years and spent those five years living outside the law, and if all I had to do was pay five grand, that's amnesty, and a great deal to boot!

History teaches us a lesson in the fall of the Roman Empire. In its heyday, the Roman Empire controlled a lot of surrounding lands. The lands are still around, but the Romans aren't. The Romans were taken over and eventually destroyed by the barbarians, the same people they had allowed to come into their territory to work for them as mercenaries, as a sort of police force for hire, doing jobs the Romans didn't want to do. Yet after the barbarians did the jobs that the Romans didn't want to do, they eventually took over the whole country. That's one of the reasons why there is no more Roman Empire. Who's to say that if we continue to allow people to come into our country to do the jobs that either we don't want to do or are too lazy to do, they won't eventually take this place over as well? It's possible that a few more generations down the line, our Western-based civilized utopia will be no more, as we're reduced to becoming a second-rate power to the Chinese. And that's where we're headed if we don't straighten things out soon.

To the ordinary working person, immigration isn't a racial issue. But I fear the federal government will make it one. For most of us, immigration is simply an issue of right and wrong, legal and illegal, fair and unfair, about people who have worked hard, paid their way, and gone through the processes legally as opposed to people who won't.

So the federal government, by whitewashing the issue, will eventually turn it into a racial issue. I'm afraid that's when Bubba is going to start thumping immigrants because he can't take it out on the federal government. He doesn't know where to find them, but he knows where to find the poor guy who's running a Weed Eater in the flower bed. It's sad when the federal government helps turn this into an even more disunited, squabbling country. But laws are real. They're tangible. You can't just sweep the laws of a society under the rug because they may be expensive to enforce. Yet our own federal government persists in doing it.

Waving the Mexican flag at me during immigration demonstrations is like waving a red flag at a bull. It pisses me off and sends the wrong message. It's as if we're dealing with a culture who, unlike the Irish or the Italians or the Greeks or the Asians or the Africans or whomever, have no reason or desire, because of the close proximity of their mother country, to truly assimilate into our culture. Instead they wave the Mexican flag in our faces at rallies, while many boxers who climb into the ring, whose lineage comes from Mexico, wear red, white and green trunks. To which I ask, if you're so proud of being a Mexican or whatever, and if you feel compelled to wave the Mexican flag or any other flag, that's fine. But why did the ring announcer say that you are now fighting out of Las Vegas, Nevada? Don't they have gyms in Mexico?

The term "anchor babies" shouldn't even be in our lexicon. There should be no such thing as a baby acting as an anchor on a chain connecting illegal family members to American social and educational programs. Neither should they act as sponsors for family citizenship once they reach age twenty-one. That's like saying if an American woman seven months pregnant goes on vacation in Europe and has the child prematurely in France, the baby's French. If instant citizenship is the result of the Supreme Court's interpretation of the Fourteenth Amendment stemming back to the Civil War, then by God the law needs to be changed. It's faulty and outdated and it's costing us billions. Even England and Australia repealed similar policies during the 1980s after numerous abuses.

As for who gets into our country and who doesn't, whether immigration is tied to letting people in with existing family members or with desirable employment skills, I say that if you've got skills that we need, then you can bring your family.

The fact remains, our immigration laws are still among the most liberal laws in the world. Countries like France, Canada, and Australia, for example, are extremely discriminating about who they let inside their boundaries. Canada, for instance, will only let in people who are skilled, employed or employable, and preferably young. Australia puts even stricter limits on the flow of immigrant family members. France is just as stern in its immigration policies.

So, with a country like the United States, which is much more desirable to live in than places like France, Canada, and Australia, why are we so anxious to pay the legal fees of lawbreaking illegals? Why are we automatically willing to grant amnesty to the tens of thousands of practicing gang members? Why do we badger our own citizens for back taxes while making no attempt to collect back taxes from illegals? The answer is simple. Instead of enforcing the laws that already exist on the books, our politicians in Washington, from the president on down, cater to corporate and ethnic-activist interests over our country's own working-class, tax-paying citizens. That is just plain wrong.

One last thing before we leave this subject . . .

Immigrant workers, legal and illegal, represent approximately 5 percent of the population of this country . . .

The unemployment rate in this country is hovering somewhere around 5 percent . . .

Hellooooo!!!

Chapter Twenty-one

POVERTY

HEN I WAS A BOY, WE'D GO OUT WEST OF TOWN A FEW miles to a lake and would go hunting and fishing. I remember seeing a straight dirt road that went through the woods. I didn't even know where it led. It just went on and on and on. The name of the road was CCC Road. I never knew what the initials stood for. My father told me the road was made back in the Depression when the government hired gangs of men who were out of work, and they would find a project for them to do or something for them to build. That's what CCC Road was about. It was a government job, and those men would go out in the woods with axes and saws and cut a road right through the middle of the Louisiana woods, just to be able to feed their families.

Nowadays there's *nobody* in this country that would be willing to do that. That kind of mentality doesn't exist anymore. The economy is so good, and we're so spoiled, we won't perform menial labor like that. If we don't have to, we won't.

The other day I read that according to the 2005 census data, thirty-seven million people in America are now living below what we call "the poverty level." That's a little less than 13 percent of our population designated as poor.

We Americans tend to feel guilty (there's that word again) because we live convenient lifestyles. I haven't been all over the world, but I have traveled a little. I went to Costa Rica one summer with my brother on a fishing trip for ESPN. (I took him because he was single and I wanted to put him on television so he could get hooked up.) I saw people who, by everyone's standards, were really poor in Costa Rica. Most Americans can't even imagine what poverty is like in a country like Mexico or Costa Rica. People literally live in shacks with walls made out of cardboard boxes and with dirt floors. Now that's poverty.

Statistically, I lived in poverty during my honky-tonkin' days. I was the bandleader playing all those clubs, and I was the guy who had to go in and sign the contracts. On paper, according to the IRS, I was making a lot of money because the clubs sent *me* all the 1099s at the end of the year. It turned out I didn't send out the appropriate forms to the other members of the band. I just threw them in the trash, so in order to settle up the tax-withholding debt, I ended up having to pay the IRS monthly for a long time. I lived "in poverty" until the tax men got every dollar outta my hide.

I have compassion for people, especially kids, who don't have things that they want, but let's put things in perspective here. Some things *are* relative. People say I'm tall at six feet, six inches. Well, if I'm standing next to Yao Ming, I'm not relatively tall at all.

Some people live below the poverty level. Whose poverty level? Okay, our poverty level. And what is our poverty level? Who sets the level? If you don't have a job where you're making enough money to support your family, yet you drive a car and live in a house that has running water and electricity and a television and modern amenities, are you living in poverty? You're still below the poverty line. That's by *our* standard. But that's not by Mexico's or Costa Rica's or India's standard. Comparatively speaking, our poor folks are rich—if not monetarily, at least in terms of opportunity.

Poor people in other parts of the world are utterly destitute. Most have absolutely nothing, and no chance of ever having anything. It's heartbreaking. But here in America, we have the freedom and the chance to break loose the chains of poverty and reinvent ourselves with opportunity that comes from education and hard work. It's never too late or impossible for an American to clean the slate and start anew.

Chapter Twenty-two

THE GRAND OLE OPRY

LOOK AT THE GRAND OLE OPRY AS A FRATERNITY. AS the story goes, the Grand Ole Opry started out as the *WSM Barn Dance*, located in the fifth-floor radio station studio of the National Life & Accident Insurance Company building in downtown Nashville. The show followed the NBC Radio Network's *Music Appreciation Hour*, which consisted of classical music and grand opera. The name came around in December 1927 when the *Barn Dance* host commented, "For the past hour, we have been listening to music taken largely from Grand Opera. Now we present the 'Grand Ole Opry.'" I guess the name stuck.

In 1943, the Opry moved to the Ryman Auditorium, where it stayed until 1974. In that year it moved to the brand-new Grand Ole Opry House, a 4,400-seater located a few miles east of downtown Nashville in the Pennington Bend of the Cumberland River. Hundreds of thousands of fans travel from around the world to see the music and comedy in person. Some of the more "contemporary" official Opry members include Clint Black, Garth Brooks, Terri Clark, Emmylou Harris, Alan Jackson, Alison Krauss, Randy Travis, Travis Tritt, Vince Gill, and Lorrie Morgan.

Playing the Opry is not like playing a standard gig. Even now, I'll go to the Opry and maybe I'll do two songs and that's it. I'll look at my schedule and if I'm home on the weekend, I'll call my manager and see if he can get us an Opry slot. Whenever I'm home I try to play the Opry. I've probably played the show fifty times or more.

The Opry today, and the current management, are trying hard to make the program more mass-appeal country. Playing the Opry is like a backyard barbecue with old friends and neighbors. You hang out backstage with other entertainers spanning the spectrum of country music. Some artists appear for the first time, with one or two singles under their belts. Then you've got Little Jimmy Dickens, who was the Garth Brooks of his day back in the fifties alongside legends like Porter Wagoner. Then there are guys like me, the men in the middle. We mingle and hang out. It's such a cool atmosphere, and it's still the longest-running live radio show in the world. The audience spans the entire country spectrum, too, from kids to blue-hairs and everyone in between. A lot of tourists and fans make the pilgrimage to Nashville just to attend a live Grand Ole Opry broadcast performance. There are two shows on Saturday night and most members make at least ten appearances a year.

When I was a kid, if you were a fan of country, you knew about the Grand Ole Opry. It was the pinnacle, and the people who were members were considered an elite group of entertainers. If you were a member of the Grand Ole Opry, you were set. Game over. You won. Your career was considered solid. The Opry was the biggest outlet for our music in the world. It had a huge radio show with a large audience, and at least as many people as the Ryman Auditorium could hold.

The Opry means different things to different people. What it boils down to for me is a love and respect for the Opry and for the legacy of country music. There's a reverence that is reserved only for that venue and no others. Being invited to become a member of the Grand Ole Opry is still an honor, because not many people are.

One night I was playing the Opry in the big Opry House. I was out onstage and I looked over to the side, and there's Little Jimmy Dickens with a stepladder. He always makes fun of how tall I am, so I always joke back at him. Like, "Little Jimmy Dickens is the only man I know where you can see his feet on his driver's license picture." After that, he came out onstage, set up his stepladder beside me, climbed to the top step where he was eye level, and asked me, "Would you like to become a member of the Grand Ole Opry?"

That's how I got invited to become a member. On August 23, 2003, I was officially inducted. The bonus was when they asked me which present member I would like to present me with the Opry Member Award, a fourteen-inch bronze and oak wood replica of the Opry's vintage microphone stand designed by renowned sculptor Bill Rains. (The wood used actually comes from the Ryman pews, which became available following the Ryman's restoration in 1994.)

I decided on Ronnie Milsap to "present me" since I'm such a huge fan of his. I feel that Ronnie opened the door for guys like me to be able to do the variety of music I'm able to do onstage and on my records and still call it country music. Whether it's country, hip-hop, R&B, or Southern rock, I love to blend different styles of music all on one album, which was something Ronnie Milsap had been doing for decades. I always like buying a Ronnie Milsap record, anticipating what the next cut is going to sound like. It's always something different and the songs seldom sound the same. The Milsap mixture somehow made sense when you put it all together onto one record. I think Ronnie was glad and excited to get the call. I know I was.

Earlier on the day of my induction, I was quoted in the newspaper as saying I would be happy to do anything the Opry asked me to do, even if it meant carrying Jimmy Dickens's guitar or cleaning Porter Wagoner's dressing room. After Milsap and the host, the beautiful Lorrie Morgan, introduced me, I did my four songs dressed in a mustard-colored suit. After I received my award, I said to the crowd, "Sometimes things happen to us that are just so good that you can't explain them, so you just have to accept them and be thankful."

But of all the times I've played the Opry, nothing surpasses my very first appearance. It was November 23, 1996, and I had released my second single from my first album. Who knew if I'd ever be invited back on that sacred stage? So I decided to ask Rhonda to marry me right there on the Opry stage. I knew I wanted to pop the question somewhere special, but I needed it to be something truly spectacular and memorable. That's how much playing the Opry meant to me. So I had my manger ask the folks at the Opry if it would be okay if I called Rhonda out and proposed to her onstage. And that's what I did. My proposal said a lot to the Opry folks, mainly, that we are family. Plus, best of all, Rhonda said yes.

Chapter Twenty-three

FATHERHOOD, KIDS, DOGS, AND MY INNER CHILD

OD IS THE ULTIMATE PRACTICAL JOKER. NOT ONLY DID he park all that oil underneath those wack-jobs in the Middle East, he saw fit to bless me with five daughters and a wife so that I'm constantly surrounded at home by females. I'm convinced that praying for a son is why I now have five girls.

I try to be a good father, like my own dad, and I want to make a conscious effort to be engaged and talk to my kids a little more. But I catch myself sometimes having gone a few days without saying anything meaningful to my daughters. I tell myself, "I guess I should speak and let them know I'm still paying attention to what's going on around the house and in their lives."

Sometimes I don't come across as a gung-ho father because I'm not that great of an actor. I can't pretend that I'm elated about all the latest kiddy events like peewee football cheerleading and ballet recitals. It's very hard for me to look excited at the dance performance that I have to attend and that I'm in charge of videotaping.

Still, I have to make an effort to act like I'm enthusiastic because I believe girls are needier than boys. They require reassurance all the time, just like women. (Basically, they're just tiny women.) There are several dramatic moments *every day* at my house. And it's usually over nothing. With that many girls under one roof, there's bound to be constant drama, and it doesn't get any better when they get older and start dating. (I have two who are at that age now.) We tried to let chivalry die in modern times, but they wouldn't let it. It's still alive because women insist on it.

With five daughters and a wife, I'm in this family-rearing job for the long haul. My kids go to public schools while my wife is busy researching their schools. She looks at the ratings and certifications of each school, to make sure that everything is cool. While I truly miss my kids when I'm on the road, I must confess I don't miss *everything*. I just miss the cute stuff. The other stuff, constantly being called on to fix things around the house or deliberate over some minor conflict—well, sometimes it's nice to be out on the road again.

The older my girls get, the more work it is for me to be a hands-on father figure. It might be different with boys. The older a boy gets, the less time is required in the parenting department, unless he's in jail or in trouble all the time. But with daughters, you are the defender of their honor until somebody else takes on that job. Regardless of how old they are, if nobody else steps in to take that gig, then it's my gig for life. I admit that sometimes I get tired of playing the role of the enforcer and having to let the older girls' boyfriends know the score.

"Okay, *I'm* here in case someone needs killin', and if you're around long enough, maybe we'll converse."

Being a twenty-first-century dad, you're supposed to be sensitive and responsive. That's hard work for me. The easy part is serving as the protector. I'm most comfortable with that role. I like being the breadwinner and working security. It's what I do best.

My old man wasn't the Great Communicator, either. It wasn't his fault. His old man was just like him. They came from generations where there wasn't all that touchy-feely I'm-OK-You're-OK communication stuff. My mother was the Great Nurturer, though, and so is my wife.

I get pressure at home that I need to be more involved with my daughters' daily lives. I'll feel guilty that I don't know specifically what's going on in each child's life at any given moment. I will ask the bottom-line questions: Is she sick? No. Is there anybody threatening her life? No. Does she have nice clothes and shoes to wear? Yes. Well, then everything's great. Right?

There are times when I can lend a helpful, objective viewpoint to everyday dramas. Here's a lesson I learned from my honky-tonkin' days. One night, my eight-year-old and five-year-old were going at it. Both of them were screaming and crying and one of them hit the other. I was lying in my bedroom watching the football game. I retreated there in fervent hope of being able to watch the game undisturbed. Then I hear my wife negotiating and trying to arbitrate between these two squabbling, tiny women. I listen for a while until finally I can't take it anymore, so I get up and become Superdad to put a stop to all this nonsense.

So I laid down the law. Everybody be quiet, including my wife. I sent the kids to their rooms and told them not to come out until I said so. I didn't yell or scream. I just told my wife to stop negotiating with the kids.

"Here's the deal. They're children! We don't care whose fault it was or wasn't, or even getting to the bottom of what the problem was. Punishment will be doled out quickly and evenly. We're looking for peace and quiet in this house. We're not searching for truth and justice. We want an immediate resolution to the conflict. I don't care who started what. I don't care who was right or wrong.

I just want them to leave each other alone until I'm through watching the football game."

Rhonda is around the girls 24/7, and it's easy to get caught up in the drama. But it's a waste of time trying to get down to a child's level and negotiate. Just send them to their rooms and then they'll learn that it doesn't matter who's right or wrong. If the peace is disrupted, they're both going to pay. I remember this bar I used to play at in Dallas that had a big sign over the entrance that said:

IF YOU START A FIGHT IN HERE, WE'LL FINISH IT.

By God, if you did start a fistfight in that establishment, you were going to get your ass kicked. It didn't matter if you beat up the guy you were fighting, the bouncers were going to stomp your ass before you left that bar and throw you out on the street.

While I'm not advocating corporal punishment, I did get spanked as a kid. About every six months, my old man gave me a good old-fashioned ass-whuppin'. Then I was a good kid until the spanking faded in my memory. Then when I acted up again, I'd get another one. I didn't get very many. If I had boys, I would probably spank them now and again. Since I have girls, it's a different thing. I don't spank my daughters.

As crazy as it sounds, raising kids is similar to breeding dogs. The reason pit bulls have the bad reputation for being vicious and dangerous is because they're owned by people who don't know how to control them. There are certain breeds of dogs that certain people should not own. If you don't have the disposition and the personality to own a pit bull, you shouldn't have one. In other words, if you're not willing to take steps to control that animal and teach him who the boss is, then you should not own that animal.

A pit bull is like a rebellious teenage boy. If you don't get his attention and show him who runs things, he's likely to get further and further out of control. You need to rein him in or he'll try to become the boss of the relationship.

Now, you can't treat a Labrador retriever that way. If you punish a Labrador retriever, it messes their brains up. It's the same with Dalmatians. If you're too tough on a Dalmatian like you have to be with a pit bull, they'll end up worthless dogs.

A lot of times, with girls, just letting them know that you're disappointed in them is enough. It breaks their hearts and they don't like to see Daddy displeased. So you can play that card with daughters.

But with boys, they don't seem to care as much.

When I was a rebellious youngster, if my father had said to me, "Daddy's disappointed in you," I would have said, "Well, Dad, I'm disappointed in me, too. I hope I don't do it again, either, but I just might."

The more success I have in my career, the more responsibility I feel toward my kids. For example, I owe it to my kids to keep on singing. If I can provide my children with a leg up and a head start in this world by getting them quality schooling, I'm gonna do it. A parent's most basic responsibility is providing an education, and since my kids are all girls, I want them to be independent. I don't want them to have to marry somebody because they need to be taken care of. I want them to be able to make their own choices and their own money, and eventually marry someone because they love them, not because they need someone to provide for them.

BEING A GOOD FATHER doesn't mean I don't have my own "inner child" to contend with. For instance, I never got to go to

Walt Disney World or Disneyland when I was a boy. Disneyland might as well have been on the moon. When we went on a vacation, if my old man couldn't drive to it pulling a camper, then we weren't going there. Whenever we'd get a couple of weeks off in the summer, we had our camper that could sleep six, and we'd hook it up behind the truck and head off to the Ozarks, in Arkansas. I loved it. We all did. Camping was our vacation. But Disneyland? Forget about it.

I do remember going to Six Flags amusement park a couple of times when I was a kid. The *real* Six Flags Over Texas. But it's not the magical place that Walt Disney World is. Six Flags is an overgrown fair while Walt Disney World is the Magic Kingdom! A truly magical place to take your kids. I love the joy on my daughters' faces whenever we all go to Walt Disney World. It sounds corny but it's true. I have to restrain *myself* to keep from running around and waving my arms over my head like I'm eight years old.

"Look! Freakin' Mickey Mouse! MICKEEEEEY!"

That's about as giddy as I ever get. And when I see my kids so excited and happy that they're about to explode, it's the best thing there is for me. That's what I like about Walt Disney World. It's a getaway for all ages. The last couple of times we've gone, we've used a personal guide, and for a certain fee they take you through the back door to all the events. We didn't have to stand in any of the long lines and all that stuff, but there's something about going in through the back door and seeing the inner workings of Walt Disney World that I really didn't need to see. No, I don't want to see Goofy clocking in on his shift, or catch Snow White and Donald Duck making out. My inner child doesn't need to see that.

Chapter Twenty-four

THE CALLING

EDUCATION AND TEACHERS . . . VERY SERIOUS PROBLEMS.
Once upon a time, in the early history of this country,
teaching was more of a "calling" than an occupation. Then, as
today, there was no huge economic dividend to becoming a teacher.
As a result, most teachers didn't get into teaching to make a lot of
money. It was almost like being a preacher. It was a calling. You
felt called to educate, to help, and to teach. And it's still is a calling to a lot of people. Yet to other people, it's about absolute job
security. "I can get this job and I don't really have to be any good
at it because they can't get rid of me."

The teachers' union has a stranglehold on the public education system. There are good teachers and mediocre teachers. The
mediocre teachers create an environment that drives good teachers away. While the unions serve to protect the mediocre teachers,
they are indirectly driving away the good teachers. (Have I mentioned my disdain for unions already?)

I love schoolteachers. I really do. But the teachers' union is one
of those scenarios where teachers are getting hamstrung by their
own organization. On an individual level, teachers are wonderful.
They're great human beings, and they're doing noble work. They
are underpaid, and most of them do try very hard. But the reason

they are underpaid is that there are a lot of stupid ones that we can't get rid of because the union is too strong. The hoops that you have to jump through to be able to get rid of a mediocre teacher are just ridiculous.

Good public school teachers have to be as frustrated as I am. The rich families have the option to go where the teachers are paid better, are performance-driven, and have a better learning environment. Vouchers are a way to give middle-class and poor parents a chance to compete. Short term, kids can cash in a voucher and the school that gets the most vouchers makes the most money. Vouchers are worth a try, if only the teachers' unions and the politicians would let us.

No Child Left Behind. Standardized national testing. Teachers have to conform to state and federal educational mandates. Some schools are unhappy about that, but perhaps a national curriculum forces the mediocre teachers to perform better so their kids can pass an objective test. Some individual instructors may not be able to figure out what nine-year-olds ought to learn. So now they have to teach those kids what the federal government says a nine-year-old should be able to learn. What that ultimately should do is expose mediocre teachers who can't take a little herd of nine-year-olds and bring them to the proper level. Then when a school district sees a certain pattern with a certain teacher who can't do as well nationally as the other classes of nine-year-olds, they know they have a problem. The teacher either needs to go back for some extra training to learn, or they have to fire that person, or maybe move that teacher back a grade or two. If those nine-year-old mental giants are too much for you, maybe you can handle the *Barney*-watching five-year-olds in kindergarten.

Some educators complain that teachers might end up only "teaching to" the standardized tests. So what? Isn't that what it's always been about? Teachers teach you for the test. We sit through a course knowing there will be some kind of test. That's what life is. We all have to take tests.

As we plod through our existences, rest assured that at the end of the line there will always be a test. "Pay attention because there's gonna be a test!" For instance, I better know the twenty songs I'm going to play tonight onstage, because at the end there's a test when ticket-buyers leave the show giving me a grade based on my performance. Somebody will always be grading you in life, so get used to it.

Another real problem in education is that we don't want our kids to fail. We don't want to admit that there are some dumb kids out there. Let's face it. Some kids are going to be laborers . . . or late bloomers . . . and we're not preparing those kids properly. We don't have shop classes anymore. I have a cousin who makes a damn good living welding. He learned to weld in high school! I took shop classes because it was fun. I remember when we had woodshop class. I learned how to work on small engines in auto shop. I learned how to grow tomato plants with the Future Farmers of America. That was important, but not so much anymore. Today there are less trade-oriented classes available while the emphasis is mainly on academics.

I don't send my kids to a private school, because the public schools in my county are the best in the state. The people who live in my county invest a lot of taxpayer resources and it's reflected in the school system. We have highly motivated parents whose kids have the benefit of intense parental interaction.

Yet that can also be an aggravating thing. In schools today, from the teachers to the students to the parents, there's an intense fear of failure. Now, for every hour of homework my kids get, we as parents are getting some homework, too.

When did all this start? I can't even imagine going home when I was in the third grade and walking up to my old man and saying, "I need you to help me do my homework." He would have looked at me and said, "Do your own homework."

Teachers now give kids projects that kids can't do alone, which means kids have to rely on parental involvement to get it done. Some schools have third-graders doing marketing assignments! For instance, my little girl had to design a wrapper on a cereal box and come up with a marketing plan, drawings, and artwork. My daughter can do the artwork, but a marketing plan for kids in the third grade?

The result is that parents jump in and help do the homework so their kids won't fail or look bad. These days, parental homework is part of a kid's education. I've spoken to parents who send their kids to private schools in our town that have *three or four hours* of homework *every night*—and I mean hands-on, parental involvement. You *have* to help the kids do these assignments. I never thought I'd see the day. Parents now have homework!

Homework used to be about reviewing what you did that day or reading the chapter for tomorrow's lesson. Prepare, practice, and review the material. Now kids are expected to learn new additional material at night. Homework is no longer just review and prepare. Now there's a teacher forcing *me,* a grown man, to do homework. Maybe they ought to send two report cards home: one for my kid, the other for me. Oops, sorry, kids, I didn't do too well this year.

It's not a major burden; it's just a pain in the butt. My wife and I are in such a fortunate position. We're blessed that neither of us has a typical nine-to-five lifestyle. We can do this and gripe about it, so it's not a huge inconvenience. But what about that working family where Mom and Dad are working nine to five, and they're

166 • TRACE ADKINS

both beat by the end of the day? They're exhausted from dealing with the rigors of work. Then they come home, feed the children, and then do two or three hours of homework before they can do the freaky-deaky and go to sleep. I don't know how they cope with it.

HERE'S A GOOD EXAMPLE of political correctness run amuck, taken to a new level by educators, teachers, and people who are supposed to be smart.

One of my girls goes to a public school where:

1. They can't have a Halloween party because it might offend Christians who think it might be a pagan holiday. So they have a "fall party."
2. They can't have a Christmas party because they're afraid it might offend somebody who's not a Christian. So they have a "winter party."
3. Needless to say, they can't have an Easter egg hunt . . . "Spring party" instead.

One week my wife was down at the school for two or three days in a row.

"So hon, what are you doing?"

"I'm working on the Mardi Gras party."

"You're working on a what party?"

"A Mardi Gras party. We're making a float."

I thought, wait a minute. Back up a second here, okay? They're having a Mardi Gras party? The same school that says they can't have a Halloween party, a Christmas party, or an Easter party? But they're having a Mardi Gras party? My wife didn't even get my ire.

Correct me if I'm mistaken, but isn't Mardi Gras a Catholic-based holiday held the day before Ash Wednesday, celebrating the final days before the beginning of Lent? The last thing you do on the day before Lent starts is do all the things you're going to give up for Lent. You raise hell. You get drunk. You eat too much. You flash your tits. You screw people you don't know. You get the idea . . . a religious holiday. Evidently, nobody thought about that. They thought Mardi Gras was something people in New Orleans do to have a big party and that it doesn't really mean anything.

Here's an idea: Let's be constant with our positions and do things consistently across the board. If we can't celebrate Christmas, Halloween . . . oh, never mind.

Here's another example of liberal-minded people trying to feel better about themselves at the expense of children.

My other daughter was in kindergarten. She came home one day and was outside when the garbage truck came by to pick up the trash. Suddenly she and her little friend came running into the house, screaming.

"The garbageman's here! He's going to kill us!"

What? I thought they were playing some kind of game. But Rhonda started asking questions. All she could get out of the kids was that the teacher had told them that there was this good man who was a king, and the garbageman killed him because he was trying to do good things for people. My wife was stumped until I figured it out.

MLK Day. Martin Luther King, Jr., came to Memphis to end the garbage strike, and he got killed. Here is my child, five years old at the time, terrified of the garbageman because someone at school decided to explain the reason for Martin Luther King Day by going into great and gory detail about the assassination of the civil rights leader.

It was another example of liberals doing things to make them feel better about *themselves*. They were just trying to do a good deed by telling these children about the injustice and the tragedy that befell the Reverend King. I guess they forgot that these kids were five years old and that all they should be expected to do is color and take naps. They are in kindergarten! Couldn't we have saved that civil rights lesson for later? Why did my five-year-old daughter need to be told that? Now she was convinced that the garbageman was out to kill her.

No disrespect to Dr. King, but leave the religion and politics to me. You teach them reading, 'riting, and 'rithmetic. Leave the rest of it to us as parents.

As far as praying in school, maybe it ought to be a majority rule thing. In my school, it was never an issue in the community. We prayed before everything. We prayed at school assemblies. Prayed before football games, prayed over the loudspeaker, and they still do. But if more parents are uncomfortable with prayer, then I guess majority rules. But I know what they do in the Muslim nations inside the madrassas. They've got no problem with praying in their schools. I guess because they're praying for all of us to be killed. Our kids are just praying for peace.

IT'S A DOG-EAT-DOG WORLD. It's survival of the fittest. One day we were driving to my wife's uncle's funeral. Daughter number three was almost three years old at the time. My wife was telling me about her uncle dying and how some in the family were going to have a really hard time because he was the main bread-winner. All that kind of serious talk. That's when my little girl blurted out from the backseat, "Every day is a test for survival."

Rhonda and I just looked at each other. Our girl was only two and a half and I guess she might have heard that on *Lady and the Tramp*. She plugged it into the conversation right where it needed to be! It was perfect. Every day *is* a test for survival. Only we've gotten so soft, impatient, and lazy, we don't have a clue how tough it used to be. We're so spoiled. We gripe about every little thing that's not right. We want it all yesterday. We want our McWorld to be McFast.

And that includes me.

I recently heard about a pill that you can take before you go to sleep that is supposed to make three or four hours of sleep feel like eight hours. As a society and as a country, we hate waiting. We want it all now. The Internet (and its instantaneous flow of information) bears a huge responsibility and I think it's an irreversible process. I can't picture us ever going back to a slower way of life.

My little kids have such great opportunities. Their minds are sharper, but they're *bored*! The result of modern organized activity and sophisticated stimuli for kids is *boredom*!

Today there's a boredom factor because children are bombarded with so much information all the time. They have to be constantly stimulated, and when they're not stimulated for thirty seconds, they're bored. When I grew up, there wasn't anything organized to do. You weren't stimulated by play groups. You got on your bicycle and you rode down the road. Maybe you ran through the woods with your friends. You fished. You created your own stimulation. Children today have to be stimulated from the outside, and when they're not, they're bored. It doesn't take long at all for that to happen.

I did something dumb the other day. Usually I'll drink my coffee however, wherever, and whenever it's ready. I don't care if it's been sitting in the pot for two days. If there's a cup of coffee left, I'll pour it in a mug and stick it in the microwave to heat it up. So there I was, standing in front of the microwave waiting. I punched in ninety seconds to heat up that cup of coffee good and hot. Except I was standing there impatiently yelling, "Come on!"

There was a day when we needed to grind up the beans, boil the water over a fire, make the coffee, no filter, with grounds at the bottom and all. Now here I was, incapable of waiting ninety seconds!

Chapter Twenty-Five

GET A REAL JOB

M Y FAVORITE PART OF MY JOB IS THE HOUR AND A HALF that I get to spend onstage a few nights a week. That's fun. No entertainer can say that applause and laughter are not food for the soul and psyche. They are. They feed you, and it's a beautiful thing.

It is also great not to have a *real* job anymore. Before I moved to Nashville, I worked in the oil fields and on drilling rigs in the Gulf of Mexico as a roustabout, a roughneck, and finally as a derrickman. When I moved to Nashville, the closest thing to that was construction, and I worked construction for about three years as a pipe fitter's helper. I had a day job until well after my first record came out in 1996.

In terms of everyday routine, my life and my standard of living have both changed pretty dramatically. The funny thing is that I miss not having a real, honest job. When I'm not touring I need a place to retreat to so that at the end of a day, I'm completely exhausted and filthy from head to toe and just stink. I need that every now and then to remind myself that I can contribute something tangible and substantial to this planet with elbow grease and perspiration.

As I write these words, my hands are so sore I can hardly make a fist. Off the road for a few days, I've been on my farm running a chain saw, swinging an ax, and clearing brush. At the end of the day, I can step back and say, "Yeah, I did something good today!" You see, the thing about the music business that is really hard for me is that there is nothing concrete to show at the end of the day. I might be busy from morning till midnight with rehearsals, interviews, and performing, but when it's all done there's nothing to look at. I've got nothing that I can put my hands on, nothing I can appreciate as far as being able to see some kind of tangible result from my efforts. It's hard for me to get that kind of satisfaction from making records because I rarely listen to them after they're done. (I'm just not that much of a fan of mine.)

That's why I like to do some hard work for a day. Then I can stand there and say, "That looks good." That's why my farm is so important to me. It keeps me sane.

Even though I'm just a journeyman in the music industry, I *am* the owner of a fairly healthy small business, operating as Sarepta, Incorporated. I couldn't think of another name, so I decided to use the name of my hometown, and they haven't sued me for it so I guess everything is okay. I have about twenty full-time employees, not counting other staff such as the management company, publicist, fan club, website, booking agency, merchandise company, transportation company, and of course my attorney. They also get checks from Sarepta, Incorporated.

Besides making records, the other part of my job is staying out on the road, playing music for my fans. It's a lot of work that incorporates a lot of folks. Sometimes I'll go out with three buses and two trucks, seven guys onstage, *plus* a guitar tech, a stage manager, a monitor guy, a front-of-house sound person, a road manager, two swag guys selling merchandise, and five drivers. For bigger shows and longer tours, I'll have as many as four buses and three trucks touring for three months straight with video screens and three camera guys and a bigger lighting rig. That's not even considered a *big* tour.

I'm easy to spot on the highway. There's a big picture of yours truly on the side of a huge semitruck that hauls most of my gear. I'll admit, it's a little embarrassing, but I understand why we do it. It's a rolling billboard. The truck carries our boards, lighting stuff, stage gear, and merchandise. I don't carry toys on the road like some other country stars do. I know guys who haul motorcycles and ATVs, but I don't do that. I'll carry a set of golf clubs and that's about it.

I've learned to have more control of my own fate. After ten years of cutting records, I retain absolute veto power over most everything in my career. In other words, nobody tells me what to do. I always try to make the right decisions with input from record label people, my managers, and my booking agent. As a result, I don't run this organization like a dictator. It's more like a democracy. Technically I'm the president of Sarepta, Incorporated, so the buck stops with me.

In the music business, the more records you sell and the more success you have, the more validity you have overall. It's not about power, it's all about validity, that you're not a fluke or a one-hit wonder, and that you know what you're doing. You have the necessary chops and endurance to know what's going on around you. You know what your fans expect and what they want to hear. After ten years of doing this job, I like to think I've got a lot of that stuff figured out.

But I can take myself too seriously. It's difficult for me to believe that I can brighten people's day simply by meeting them before or after a show. It's really hard for me to accept that, because I'm modest, sometimes to a fault. I know my limitations, I know just how good I really am: I'm an okay singer, an okay entertainer, and realize that maybe I was just in the right place at the right time. I got my shot mostly because I wouldn't go away. I refused to quit. But I guess there's a lot about being a star that I still don't get.

I know there are a lot of musicians out there who would love to have a gig like mine. They would love to be touring and playing their own music. I admit it, it's a great job. But what we do is not hard or complicated. Compared to most working folk, this is recess, man. We're playing music, for God's sake. Once you master your instrument or your singing voice, then everything else is gravy.

The Trace Adkins management style is simple and direct. I expect people to do their jobs without being told what to do. Micromanaging is not my thing; I'm all about delegating responsibility. I do things the way we used to when I worked offshore. Everybody was expected to take care of their specific duties, and that's all I expect any of my employees to do now. Do your job without me having to constantly tell you what that job is, and you'll be able to work for me as long as you want to. If somebody does really well, I give them the necessary pat on the back. If I have to always point things out or take you by the hand, I don't have the patience for that. I don't have a problem giving someone all the responsibility they can handle, up to the point of them doing *my* job. But then again, if you think you can do my job better and I don't have to show up at all, then I will have achieved ultimate success.

Oh, by the way . . .

If any industry people read this and scoff at my elementary explanations of the music business, or if you say under your breath, "This guy's a moron." . . .

. . . You're an asshole.

Chapter Twenty-six

A COUNTRY BOY . . . STILL

M Y FARM IS ABOUT FORTY MILES SOUTH OF NASHVILLE, and about twenty miles from my house. It's in a little rural town, not unlike Sarepta. I can go twenty miles to get a million miles away. My whole spread is sixty acres, forty-five of which are and were woods. There are about ten acres I need to keep up and there's a hill in the back that spreads out into the woods. I've built a couple of new barns and I've got a four-acre pond. Someday I plan to build a small cabin out there for my ultimate getaway. Meanwhile, inside one of the barns, there's electricity and plumbing with a separate private room where I can recharge. It's not the Ponderosa, but it's enough for me.

My farm is my sanctuary. It's a place where I go to do that hard physical work I was talking about to make myself feel like a worthwhile human being again and to feel like I'm making a difference. I go there to contemplate. Make tough decisions. Clear my head. When I'm out there by myself running a saw, swinging an ax, or riding a tractor, that's where I figure everything out. I can solve the world's problems and a few of my own.

I don't bring my work out there. I don't write songs on the farm. Instead I fish in my pond, which we've stocked with bass, bluegill, and channel cat. Most of the neighbors know me, but they're cool and give me my space. I've done most of the cleaning up, clearing the trash, cutting the brush, and trimming the trees by myself. I've also physically moved enough rocks to impress a prison chain gang. It's a place I'm extremely proud of.

When I first found the property, my wife thought I had lost my mind. It was all grown over and had been part of an old three-hundred-acre dairy farm that hadn't been worked on for over twenty years. It was in a terrible state. There was no fence around the property. There was just a little creek that ran through a valley with piles of garbage all along the hillside. The land had remnants of a house that had burned down, and a few dilapidated buildings—a tobacco barn, a dairy barn, another old shed, and a chicken house. There was trash everywhere because people had been using it as a dump. However, once I saw the spring coming out of the side of that hill, and I could see how the land lay down in the valley, I knew what it would look like if I could get my hands on it and work the land. I had originally envisioned buying fifty acres somewhere in Tennessee, a relatively square plot of land where I could build a house right in the center. I wanted a spring and a big hill. I could see that this was, topographically, exactly what I was looking for. I called up Rhonda all excited.

"I found the place!"

The first time I brought my wife out to see the farm, she started crying. "Oh my God, what are you doing?"

I tried to explain. "Stay with me here. This is what I see: the pond, two barns, with a beautiful farmhouse and a winding gravel road up to the top of the hill."

Sometimes wives just can't visualize stuff like that, yet I could see it like it was already done. I could see the potential of the place once it was cleaned up. Today, it's well on its way to becoming the gorgeous property I saw in my mind's eye. If you could see a before-and-after picture, you'd have trouble believing it was even the same place. I'm so glad that Rhonda trusted my judgment and supported my vision.

I work a lot out there now. I've hired a few people to help me out and brought in heavy equipment to build and dredge the pond and use the dirt fill and crushed rock to build roads. I've cleared most everything else by myself with chain saws and tractors.

When I'm not on the road or in the studio, I'm usually out on the farm scaling back tree branches, burning brush, and cleaning stuff up. It's a marathon process, but I'm winning the fight.

You see, I need my farm to offset the craziness of making music and being on the road. Like I said before, outside of being onstage for ninety minutes, I find it hard to see tangible results at the end of the working day from just being a singer. People dismiss me when I mention that to them. But it's true. Once you sing a song, it's gone.

"Can't you see the smiles you put on the people's faces in the audience?" they ask me, incredulously. "That's what you do. That's your reward and your tangible results."

But it's not enough. I need a place to get away from the world so I can contemplate the world.

A country boy needs a place to be a country boy.

Chapter Twenty-seven

CIGARETTES AND COFFEE

TOBACCO WAS AMERICA'S FIRST CASH CROP. EVEN TODAY, I pass tobacco fields on the drive from my house to my farm. I started to chew as a kid and I remember my first dip of snuff. It made me so dizzy, I fell and hit my head on a doorknob. I still carry the scar on my forehead. When I started using tobacco as a youngster, my father, who used to be a smoker, tried to discourage me. He warned me not to get hooked. "Trace," he'd say, "don't even start, son." But pretty soon I was stealing cigarettes from him.

I really don't want to smoke anymore, but I *really* enjoy it. It's a simple pleasure. Being a man with ideals from the nineteenth century, I love tobacco. I love to chew it *and* smoke it.

There's nothing like the taste of a Marlboro. If I have to bum a smoke and someone gives me something light, I'll break off the filter and try to smoke it. But I need my pack of Cowboy Killers.

I'm not what you'd call a gourmet tobacco consumer. I'm not big on pipes or imported cigarettes, and I don't go for hand-rolled cigars. I feel the same way about coffee, whiskey, and beer. I never cared which brand I drank. When I drank, all I cared about was the proof. Was it hundred proof? That'll work. I drank lots of beer with a small "b." Not too much dark beer, though I do like my coffee black, strong, and hot, as long as it's not decaf. And I don't drink coffee for the taste. I drink it for the effect, the same reason I drank whiskey and beer.

I don't smoke in restaurants. In fact I think it's kind of funny when I go into a restaurant and they ask if I want to sit in the smoking or nonsmoking area. It doesn't matter, because I'm not going to smoke anyway. I didn't come here to smoke. I came here to eat. As soon as I'm done eating, then I'll go outside and burn one.

You can't smoke in a bar in California. And in New York City, you can't smoke in a bar, a pool hall, an OTB parlor, a bowling alley, or even your company car. A smoking ban in a bar is the epitome of ridiculous. Think about it. You're talking about a place where 99.9 percent of the patrons aren't going there for their health. Outside of a few wine drinkers looking for antioxidants, nobody, including the employees, goes into a bar with the intention of doing anything healthy to their bodies. So while I'm giving myself cirrhosis of the liver, don't you dare blow any secondhand smoke in my face!

If I could press a button and instantly quit, I certainly would. I've tried the patch, the pill, even the gum. I think there comes a time in a man's life when he looks in the mirror one day and decides enough's enough. Then he quits. That's exactly what my old man did, and I'll probably do the same. No sooner. No later.

Meanwhile, as the sin tax on tobacco continues to soar, it's obvious that we smokers remain the whipping boys of society. I often ask myself, why can't I enjoy my tobacco in peace? And don't give me that bullshit about secondhand smoke. That's statistical crap. So if I'm such a burden to our health care system, how come nobody says anything to the 350-pounder who walks into Burgers "R" Us and orders up a couple of double cheeses, an extra-large order of fries, and a tanker truck full of Coke? Nobody's charging her an extra forty-cent sin tax on fast food. What if whenever you walked into McDonald's there was a chart posted at the register, and if your height and weight didn't match up, you were required to pay a fat tax, with all the proceeds going toward fighting childhood obesity? People would raise holy hell!

All in all, I'm ultraconsiderate about my smoking. When I'm outside, I always "field strip" my butts. That is, I'll twist off any leftover tobacco and stash the butt in my pocket. I never smoke in the car with my children. I never smoke in my house. I never smoke in anybody else's house or car, and I won't even ask, unless they're smoking. But I'll still draw the line if and when they pass a law banning smoking outdoors. I swear, I will stand next to the sign and smoke until they haul me off to jail. Then I'll hire a hotshot lawyer and together we will challenge the constitutionality of whether or not a red-blooded, taxpaying American citizen is allowed to peacefully smoke outside. I'm convinced my smoking in a seven-acre park isn't hurting anybody. And I don't need the government trying to protect me from myself.

Now some geniuses want to give an R rating to a motion picture if somebody in it smokes a cigarette. The suits at NBC must have been sobbing uncontrollably as Angel Cabrera played the last two holes of the U.S. Open smoking like a man who was about to be executed. Since I smoke, does that automatically mean I lead an R-rated life? All in all, I feel bad about smoking. Sometimes I'll be sitting out on the deck smoking a cigarette, and my two-year-old will be standing there looking at me, watching the smoke curl up in the air. That's what makes men kick the habit.

THE OTHER DAY at the airport I needed a cup of coffee. I got behind a guy who ordered something like a vanilla double soy latte or whatever with this, that, and the other thing. I was thinking, Damn dude, just let me squeak by and get my cup of black coffee and I'll be out of y'all's way.

This gave me an idea.

I should open up a little kiosk.

Call it "Just Joe."

Just coffee.

A big cup or a little one. That's your choice.

Ask for anything else, and we'll have the same attitude as the Soup Nazi on *Seinfeld*. "No coffee for you. Get out!"

Black coffee.

If you want sugar and stuff, it's around the corner over at that Starbucks.

No muffins.

No pastries.

No souvenir cups.

No candy.

No aprons.

No T-shirts.

No hats.

No CDs.

Just a good strong cup of coffee.

If that's what you're into, we can hook you up.

Just Joe.

Chapter Twenty-eight

SIXTEEN ACRES: WELCOME TO HELL

THEY TOLD ME I WAS THE FIRST COUNTRY ARTIST TO VISIT Ground Zero in New York City after 9/11. It was only two weeks after the Twin Towers went down, and things were still burning, smoking, and smoldering. The official response had just been downgraded from rescue to recovery.

It was an eerie experience walking down the street toward Ground Zero, one I'll never forget. I couldn't quite see the site as I walked past the buildings that were between me and where the World Trade Center once stood. They had cleaned everything up on the ground so you didn't really know how close you were to Ground Zero until you looked up and saw fiberglass and paper and other debris still stuck in the trees. Wicked.

Before I got to the site, I found it hard to get a true sense of how big that area really was. Sixteen acres of New York City! Once I got there, I simply couldn't take it all in. I had to pan my eyes across a long terrain in order to take it all in. It was that vast. The weight and the gravity of it wasn't lost on me. As I stood there, I soaked in every little detail as the sight of Ground Zero seared into my memory. I never wanted to forget the sights, the sounds, or the smell. It was an odd combination of several smells, kind of like a burning clutch. We've all smelled burning wood, plastic, even hair, but never all together.

There were lots of people milling around and staring thoughtfully down from street level into the abyss, but everybody was quiet and still as the excavation process continued. There was an eerie peacefulness about the place. I knew that people's remains were scattered among the debris, and that left a chill inside me. Another feeling inside was the knowledge that Ground Zero was a shrine, a place to pay homage to how fleeting and unpredictably short life could be at any given moment.

I gazed sadly at all the destruction until we left and boarded a Navy hospital ship that was docked nearby. I walked on deck and it was one of the strangest experiences I've ever had. I was supposed to be there just shaking hands, saying thanks, and keeping morale up, but I felt like I was in the way. I felt like I needed to put on a hard hat and a pair of gloves and go out to the site and physically help.

I shook hands and hugged guys for what seemed like hours. When it came time to leave, I asked if I could have one last look at the site. It was almost more than one human mind could absorb. Our ability to grasp the larger scheme of things is finite, just as it's difficult to comprehend the notion that the universe goes on and on forever. We can't perceive eternity. But for me, it was equally difficult to comprehend those sixteen acres of total devastation. I don't care how many times the cameras flew over; you can never experience the full impact from the television coverage. It doesn't affect you patriotically the way it does when you're standing there seeing it or smelling it. It wasn't a horrible odor, nothing pungent, deathly, or offensive. It just smelled like destruction.

A farmer just south of Nashville illustrated it best. He was so moved he put together a tribute to 9/11 by planting more than three thousand white wooden crosses, spread out over sixteen acres. It was an amazing and tangible example of how vast the destruction of 9/11 really was.

After my visit I immediately put pen to paper. I wrote a song with Bobby Terry that may be the best song I've ever written. The lyrics flowed out of me while Bobby played some swampy guitar licks. I was very angry as we wrote. I heard the dark mood of the song in my head and Bobby gave me exactly what I wanted. (He's one of the best guitar players I know.) While everyone else was writing mainly patriotic songs, I wanted to take it to a darker, more sinister place. After those gut-wrenching feelings I experienced at Ground Zero, it struck me as bizarre and ludicrous that these fanatical Muslims actually believed (and devoutly so) that after committing those horrible atrocities that they would end up in heaven with seventy-two virgins.

So I thought, You know what? Somebody needs to write a song from the Devil's point of view, welcoming these assholes to hell. That's how I wrote it, speaking in first person as the Devil to one of the 9/11 hijackers:

Come on in, son, have a seat
Don't mind the screams, don't mind the heat
It's been like this 'round here for a long, long time
We haven't had the chance to meet
But I've heard about you on TV
And I think we're gonna get along just fine
I can't help but notice
You look somewhat surprised
Did you think, son, after what you've done,
The Lord would let you slide?

Welcome to Hell, your new home
You did the crime now you'll do the time
Right where you belong
Welcome to Hell, end of the line
Your final sin, got you in
And now your soul is mine
Welcome to Hell

> "Welcome to Hell,"
> by Trace Adkins and Bobby Terry

In my opinion, when we hit Afghanistan in retaliation for 9/11, we shouldn't have pulled the trigger until we had a million boots on the ground lined up from the extreme northwest portion of the country to the extreme northeast. And once we had those half a million soldiers positioned, we could have just started marching south like Sherman's army. Just cleaning up, annihilating every Taliban stronghold we came across.

That would have taken us to the Pakistan border, at which point a phone call to General Pervez Musharraf would have sounded like, "All right, you saw what we just did in Afghanistan? Now, we'll give you a week to find bin Laden and his gang. Meanwhile, we'll sit right here and sharpen our bayonets and clean our guns. If at the end of that week you haven't exterminated him, we're going to do it."

Maybe that's the way it should have been handled. That's the no-quarter approach Nathan Bedford Forrest would have undertaken. I don't care if other people say, "That just brings us down to their level," because that's the only level these people understand. They don't care about diplomacy or compromise. They view that as weakness. We needed to go into Afghanistan and be just as merciless and brutal as they were with us.

That's the only way to fight these radical Muslims today. Historically, they only respect raw physical power. Trying to fight a sanitized, precisely targeted, politically correct, compassionate war is just not intelligent. It doesn't work. I mean, my God, didn't we learn that in Vietnam? You either go in with your best team on the field or you don't play the game. In Afghanistan and Iraq, we're mobilizing our soldiers like they're police officers, which is crazy.

Sadly, the American public at large has little personal stake in our campaigns in Iraq and Afghanistan. It's as if the government is saying, "Don't worry, we have an all-volunteer army to take care of this mess. Carry on with what you're doing." We haven't been asked to sacrifice a thing. We have, however, been warned against "profiling" to avoid violating anyone's civil rights.

For that reason, I fear we're still vulnerable to another 9/11-style attack. There are most likely enough sleeper cells in this country, and probably more in Canada, to cause more major disasters unless we wage this antiterrorist fight more effectively. It's not hard at all to cross our borders from Mexico and Canada. We've only recently required passports for exit and entry.

History repeats itself and it infuriates me. We have been at war with radical Islam since we became a young country! We started having our clashes with militant Muslims two hundred years ago. Listen to "The Marine's Hymn," written in the nineteenth century: "To the shores of Tripoli." You remember Tripoli, the de facto capital of Libya.

After the Revolutionary War, in 1796, we were developing trade with the other countries across the Atlantic. However, pirates from Tripoli attacked our ships, stole our goods, and kidnapped our crews. That resulted in the First Barbary War, which dragged on for four years until a treaty was signed in 1805.

First we tried paying a ransom, eighty-three thousand dollars a year, nearly 10 percent of our national budget, to the Muslim pirates so they would leave us alone. That worked for a few years before they were back at it again, looting and plundering our ships in the Mediterranean Sea. The Second Barbary War followed because they reneged on the deal . . . they always do. We should have learned then that peace and security can't be purchased with cash.

Radical Islamists—then and now—want to kill *us* and everybody else who is not a Muslim. That is their mantra. Their edict. Their mission. It's the burden that's been given to them by the prophet Muhammad. Kill every infidel who is not of like mind, and who doesn't believe as you do. If we would only make a mass conversion to Islam, then maybe they'd let up.

Representative Keith Ellison of Minnesota became the first Muslim elected to Congress and was sworn into office with his right hand on the Koran instead of the Bible. And whose copy of the Koran was it? It was Thomas Jefferson's. Ellison cited that Thomas Jefferson had read the Koran, but that's only half the story. Thomas Jefferson *did* own a copy of the Koran, all right. But why did he own a copy? President Jefferson wanted to know why it was that the Muslims hated us. He couldn't figure it out, because we hadn't done anything to them. We hadn't instigated warfare or wronged them in any way that Jefferson could see. So he picked up a copy of the Koran to read, to try to figure out why. In that copy of the Koran, Jefferson got his answer. He finally understood why they hated us, and that they always would. He was correct because evidently, they still do.

So you see, we've been in conflict with these people for over two hundred years. Sometimes it's been in a covert way, sometimes in open warfare. There's never been a meeting of the minds between us and radical Islam, and there never will be. Ever. People today who preach so-called tolerance don't get it. Liberal politicians, who seem to be suggesting that we pay and appease these rogues, are simply advocating that we repeat history.

Israel has certainly learned that negotiating with terrorists is futile. They are surrounded by enemies who pray for their destruction. In addition to hostile governments, they now have to contend with Muslim street gangs like Hezbollah in Lebanon and Hamas in Palestine. Israel, however, is perfectly capable of defending itself if we would allow it to do so. The Israelis are like a pit bull at the end of a chain standing on its hind legs, foaming at the mouth, wanting to attack somebody every time they're provoked. Luckily, for the rest of the Middle East, we've got a firm grasp of the other end of the chain. Take this Iranian nuclear mess, for example. I don't worry about it because as soon as Iran's nuclear capabilities become operational, Israel will send a few bombs down the smokestack, and it'll be all over. Don't we Americans remember recent history, when during in the early 1980s the Israelis blew up Iraq's nuclear capabilities? Well, they'll do it again in Iran.

I say let's all be realists, not racists, about the volatility in the Middle East. I think sometimes people get those two concepts, racism and realism, mixed up. I'm not a racist, just a realist. It's not that we have anything against Arab and Persian people, or people with darker skin. It's just some of their philosophies that we dislike. Some of us understand that some of *them* want to kill all of *us*, and our children.

Let me put it another way. If two little Muslim children somehow ended up on my doorstep one morning, hungry, cold, and naked, I promise you I would take those children in and feed and clothe them, and try to solve whatever problem had caused them to be in this condition. I would do that in a heartbeat.

Now, let's turn the tables. If my blond-haired, blue-eyed little girls ended up on some radical Islamic goatherd's doorstep one morning, naked and hungry, what would he do for them?

I don't even want to think about it.

Chapter Twenty-nine

THE ELEPHANT AND THE CHIHUAHUA

TOO MANY AMERICANS HAVE A POSTAGE-STAMP-SIZED view of our foreign policy. Too few are stepping back to look at the big picture. We're not acknowledging the proverbial elephant standing in the living room. We don't want to admit he's there, but there he is. Swinging his trunk around, knocking people down and destroying the furniture. He's bellowing and trumpeting, but still nobody pays any attention to him.

That elephant is Islam.

We live in a world where Islamic extremists think that Western society has corrupted the planet, so they've vowed to stop us, and shut down our influence. It's not enough for us just to leave them alone, and to walk away from them or pay them off by buying their oil at exorbitant prices. Islamic fundamentalist extremists and their Al-Qaeda henchmen are bound and determined to kill as many of us as they can, anywhere they can, whenever they can, and not just Americans. They want to kill anyone who embraces Western culture and Western civilization.

Excuse me for mixing my metaphors, but these people are also like a tiny little dog that one of my aunts once had. I now know why God made Chihuahuas only four pounds: because if they were ninety pounds, they'd be the baddest, most dangerous four-legged creatures on earth. Aunt Betty Jo's (now there's a country name for ya) Chihuahua thought he was an African lion. I'd walk in and that mongrel would attack my ankles as if he was seriously trying to chew my leg off. He thought he was really going to do some damage, but instead he was just an annoying pain in the ass. He wasn't drawing blood, but he sure was aggravating. That's what the Islamic extremists are like. They're just Chihuahuas chewing on our ankles and making our lives miserable. While they're not doing any real economic or social damage lately, they're keeping us pissed off all the time and on edge.

We need to get past this, and I'm afraid it's going to come down to something later that we don't have the stomach to do today. It's going to take brutality to stop Islamic terrorism and that's the only way we're going to curtail it. Unfortunately, we may never resort to such tactics, which could be to our detriment. I don't claim to be an authority on Islam, but I think I know all I need to know. Some people, including President Bush, have, in an attempt to be diplomatic, assured us that Islam is a religion of peace. Uh . . . okay.

Now, I agree that unconditionally condemning Islam would be like saying that all Christians are radicals because of the actions of a few "crazies." I've often heard liberals say that Christianity has its own extremists. They point to some so-called Christians waving signs that say "God Hates Fags," or those nuts who blow up abortion centers and kill doctors in the name of God.

However, here's the "but."

We know that 99.999 percent (that may be a little high) of the Christians in this country are law-abiding, fine, upstanding, hard-working citizens, and that only a tiny percentage of the extremists, way out on the fringe, carry things too far. We also know that radical Christians haven't declared war on Islam and haven't started killing Muslims in this country just because God told them to. But that's what Islamic extremists are doing in several parts of the world. They kill Jews and Christians in the name of Muhammad as they pursue jihad, a radical religious philosophy of holy war that started out in Egypt and spread all the way to Afghanistan and Pakistan and all points in between.

To me that's a big difference. We don't have Christian and Jewish extremists flying planes into buildings in Islamabad, although I could almost understand why some Christians and Jews would hate Islamic extremists enough to resort to those means. And, who knows, it may come to that someday, but not until it becomes so unbearable that our hand is forced. Although I can't picture it escalating to Christian suicide bombers, I fear that someday somebody is going to take it upon themselves to get some personal payback, right in the Islamics' own backyard, just like in the Crusade days. We didn't start this war against Islamic extremists, but somebody needs to finish it, whether it's us or our children's children.

So maybe we shouldn't look at the postage-stamp-sized view of Iraq in the extreme short term. What may come out regarding our whole Iraq conflict was our need to establish a beachhead. The "real" purpose for the invasion may have been to establish a permanent Middle East base of operations that we control, strategically positioned to deal with problems when they flare up. We can just zoom in and nip it in the bud, get it under control, and retreat back to base. A base of operations where our troops, supplies, munitions, and firepower are close by when we need them. Is that what we were trying to accomplish all along in Iraq? If so, I wish the White House had been straight with us and admitted it.

People often wonder why we must always resort to military intervention. Why can't we bomb the Middle East with Western culture, our music, technology, and positive aspects of our contemporary way of life? I say we're already doing that in a de facto way. That's why the fundamentalist Muslims (with money pouring in from Saudi Arabia) have set up the madrassas (schools where they teach Muslim children to hate) all over the Middle East, Pakistan, and Afghanistan. The hard-liners of Islamic culture are scared shitless that Western culture is going to pervade their society, and corrupt the splendid utopian Garden of Eden they've created in the desert countries they live in. Maybe they're afraid that we're going to turn their arid kingdoms into Las Vegas–like desert communities.

Fortunately, we *can* win the cultural war through commerce with larger and more important countries, such as China and India. Whenever China and India see change taking place, they react by rolling with the capitalistic flow in a big way. They're playing the game by concluding that Western influence (read: dollars) may not be so bad for their society and economy after all. The Chinese and the Indians are smart and forward-thinking people. Unlike the Islamics, they're not trying to drag the rest of the world back into the seventh century.

Still, it's disturbing to see children in madrassas in Pakistan brainwashed from the time they're three years old to believe all the lies about us. From the time they can walk, extremists' kids are taught that America is the enemy, and that we are the devils to hate. Yet we don't raise our children that way. We don't teach our children to hate Muslims like that.

If anybody wonders who the good guys are and who the bad guys are in this world, just look at it that way. Look at the way we teach our children as opposed to the way they teach their children. The point is there are hard-line fundamentalists in the Muslim world who are scared to death of the influence of Western culture in their countries, so the extremists react.

One last thing . . .

The elephant is also scared of the Chihuahua.

Chapter Thirty

LAYING HATE: NO MERCY, NO QUARTER

THE ONLY TIME I'VE EVER BEEN OVERSEAS WAS WHEN I went to the Persian Gulf in the fall of 2002, and it was a life-changing experience. We were contacted by the USO, a fine organization that helps, immeasurably, our troops and their families. Anything that I have ever done with the USO has been a spiritually rewarding endeavor.

We (myself, my manager, and three band members) boarded a plane in Nashville, flew to New York, then on to Amsterdam, Dubai, and eventually Bahrain.

When you land on the deck of an aircraft carrier and grab that tailhook—man, they don't make a ride like that in any amusement park. It's an awesome experience!

We played in the hangar down below, on the aircraft carrier *Abraham Lincoln*. It was a thrill, and one of the highlights of my career. The troops were so appreciative, and they seemed to hang on every note we played. It's an honor to have so many country music fans in uniform. This was shortly before the launch of Operation Iraqi Freedom, so I got to write messages on several bombs. After we got back home, a month later, I was watching the news footage and knew that some of those bombs had my name on them.

We flew in a prop plane, the same kind they use to haul the

mail and bring out fresh personnel. It wasn't a jet, so when they shot us off the deck I thought we were going to crash because the catapult sends you out much faster than the plane can actually fly. So when it slows down to its normal flight speed, it feels like you're going in the drink. At least it felt that way to me.

Before we took off, the pilot told me, "If you want the best seat, sit in the very back and completely relax your body." When you sit in the back, you're facing backward, and there's nothing behind you but open space in the back of the plane. So when it takes off, you can't help yourself. Your feet and hands are extended. Your head's down. It's a rush!

We played a naval base first, then went out and performed on the aircraft carrier, and then we appeared at an Air Force base right on the edge of the Kingdom of Bahrain. And they have a lot of nerve to call Bahrain a kingdom. It's just a desert island with one tree in the middle of it. Later we got the privilege to tour a Los Angeles–class nuclear powered attack submarine on the Persian Gulf. Unlike my bus, I certainly couldn't live on one of those submarines. I'd go absolutely nuts. It's too tight, too small, and, besides, I'm too tall. Submarines were not designed for tall sailors. The captain's quarters were about the size of a normal walk-in closet. Everything just seemed cramped. However, it is an incredible piece of equipment.

The men and women that we met on that USO trip were an absolute inspiration. They renewed my sense of pride to be an American. I was forewarned by Mr. Wayne Newton that I would feel that way. I had an opportunity to speak with him before we left so I asked him what to expect.

Wayne said, "Trace, you will probably feel guilty when you come home because you'll feel as if they gave you more than you gave them."

I wasn't sure what he meant at the time.

I am now.

I DON'T KNOW how I'd hold up in a war effort, seeing the way our country wages war these days. If I were a soldier in Iraq, I'd probably last two weeks before they would have to send me home. I'd be gung-ho like I was roughneckin' on the Gulf of Mexico. I would go out on patrol every day and then I'd have to go to the quartermaster or the provisions people for more bullets. It would be a free fire zone every time I'd be out on patrol. I'd be busting a lot of caps. I wouldn't give a damn; let them throw me in the stockade. I would come to Baghdad to kick ass.

But the politicians are micromanaging the show now in Iraq. The military leaders are no longer really in charge of what's going on in the Middle East. That's the reason our boys are getting killed: the Iraqis don't respect us. Now that the Beltway bureaucrats are in charge, things are incredibly screwed up, and they are going to remain so until we let the military take over again and do the things that need to be done. Start making examples of how it's got to be! Start waging war even if it's going to be ruthless, blood-curdling, and bloodletting! That's what needs to happen.

The Democrats won't vote down the money that finances wars, because they know that if they did, they would lose the American people altogether. The American people want to end conflicts and send our troops home, but they don't want Congress to "cut and run." They want to find another way. The problem the Democrats have is that since they don't have their man sitting in the Oval Office, the only tool that's left to them is the purse, and if they cut off the money, it could be spun that the Democrats don't support our troops. I can understand their frustrations. We as conservatives have our own frustrations. Nobody has a clear mandate, and only a slim majority. It's enough to maintain gridlock but not enough to be decisive and take action.

Most Americans are opposed to the Iraq War because it's perceived that we're not *winning* the war. They're not pissed about why we're fighting. They're just starting to see Iraq as Vietnam, Part II, and we've got to change that.

Some Americans still don't believe that Iraq is a real war. Conservatives are frustrated because most people don't understand that we're actually at war. Make it look like we're in a war—and fight it like a war, not a police action! A lot of public opinion has to do with the information we're getting. Right now we only know how many of our beloved American troops have died.

Here's an example. It would be hard for a collegiate athletic program to continue operating if the only thing that ever made it into the papers was the games they lost. If their victories were never printed, pretty soon they'd look like a pretty crappy team. Nobody would support the team monetarily. Nobody would go to the games if all they heard about were the losses.

We Americans love winners. In addition to our own casualties, we want to know what's happening to the other side. If we knew more about what we were doing right, you'd see a marked difference in the support of the war. If only the American people got the word that we'd won one every now and again. But instead, we're barraged daily with grim news and American casualties with no word on the impact we're making on the enemy.

A day of reckoning is coming when we'll have to address the problem. We can either deal with it now or our kids are going to inherit the debacle down the road—along with the debt we're piling up staging a half-assed campaign. Somebody's going to have to fight this fight! We can choose to do it now or later, but eventually it's coming to a head in that region.

Should we have gone into Iraq in the first place? Not if we weren't ready to fight to win and get medieval on the enemy. If we aren't ready to do the job, then don't go. We've been in Iraq going on five years, and we've lost almost four thousand soldiers with more than seventy thousand soldiers injured. Yet when you realize we took twenty-six thousand casualties at Iwo Jima alone, I doubt if this country is ready to deal with that kind of sacrifice. But we must.

When you go into a fight, and one guy's wearing brass knuckles, you don't step in the ring with sixteen-ounce boxing gloves on. But that's the way we now fight in the modern era. We've got precision bombs and all that dazzling video-game-style weaponry. Not to protect our ground forces, but to prevent collateral damage! We as a country are so damned compassionate, concerned, and scared that we're going to make somebody mad, we spend billions of dollars trying to make sure we can send a rocket down some radical Islamist's chimney so that we don't hurt his neighbor who's out trimming his date palm trees. That's the problem. If we're going to go to war, we have to let our troops kill people. That's the ugly truth. You must step into the ring with your game face on and fight to win, and win convincingly, leaving your opponent lying there beaten to a bloody pulp. You leave no doubt, and that's the way war needs to be conducted. It's not as if we don't have troops who are brave and tough enough to administer the beating. Our boys have been ordered to hold back, and that outrages me.

I was working on my farm with a young man from Special Forces. It was so refreshing to hear about our current situation from his perspective. He actually *wanted* to go back to Iraq after two tours of duty. According to him, there was more drama over here regarding the war than there is over there. It's the everyday bullshit *over here* that gets on his nerves a lot worse than having Iraqi militants throwing hand grenades at him. According to him, during the first two years or so of the conflict, our boys didn't have to put up with that crap. They got up in the morning, went to chow, and then they'd go out on patrol. They knew what their jobs were, nobody messed with them, and they did their thing. Now things have drastically changed, and not for the better.

Once our troops were "urged" to stop killing, and were basically told to start acting like elementary school crossing guards, we began suffering casualties. As the civil war escalated with the bombing of the Shiite golden mosque by the Sunnis, our men became referees trying to keep the peace. Once that happened, things started unraveling. My young friend told me that the last time he killed an Iraqi insurgent in battle he was interrogated for three days! Why do we persist in holding our troops back and not allowing them to do what they should be doing?

I SAID EARLIER, as a Civil War buff I admire the tactics of Nathan Bedford Forrest, the Confederate officer who invented what we now call "the moving offense." He never had the opportunity to attend a military academy, and he never formally studied battle tactics. He fought using his own common sense and an ability to exploit man's fear of death. He knew that fear was a tool that could be used as an advantage, to literally scare the shit out of your enemy.

He could take 500 members of his cavalry and charge 2,500 enemy riders and scare them so badly, they'd turn and run. His reputation had gotten such that if you came up against him on the battlefield, you never knew what to expect. How was he feeling today? Would he charge? How would he fight? The Union officers didn't know.

Forrest learned to use his reputation to *save* lives. The tactic he employed was to surround a garrison and send in a trooper under a flag of truce with a list of demands. He would ask for surrender and add that if he were forced to attack, no quarter would be given. In other words: Everybody dies. It worked every time save one.

We can't play that game today for a couple of reasons: 1) We don't have the stomach for it. 2) Our enemies know that.

War could be avoided altogether if we still had that "sleeping giant" reputation that we had in World War II; but we don't, and the Vietnam conflict is to blame.

We can all blame Winston Churchill for the Iraq War. He set up Iraq in the first place. As the story goes, after World War II, France and Britain fought over pieces of the Middle East. The Brits grabbed Palestine and then combined all the puppet factions that hated each other and created the unstable kingdom of Iraq. It probably didn't make sense back then, just as it doesn't make sense now. Perhaps it never will.

The big problem now is oil. You can't split up the country into separate religious factions because certain regions will have oil while certain regions won't. On top of their religious differences, oil gives them more reason to hate and kill each other. Therein lies the problem.

Today I often wonder, do our enemies fear and respect us, or do they see us as peacekeepers and cops on the beat? The American people are sick of how this war is being run. Yet I believe that if an urgent call to arms was issued, the response would be overwhelming. Imagine a million hardcore, pipe-swinging roughnecks itching to bust heads. You wouldn't have enough uniforms to put on the sons of bitches who would step forward for a tour of duty.

If you told the American people that we were not going to appease or make friends, but instead were going to fight an all-out war, who would want to go? I believe that call would be answered.

If you look back in history, especially to the Civil War, the intensified killing started when the forty-year-olds got involved in the fray. With the Napoleonic tactics that were generally employed, both sides suffered up to 30 percent casualty rates in almost every battle! Eventually, after the military went through their pool of eighteen- to twenty-five-year-olds, they started taking guys over the age of thirty.

A young soldier in his late teens or early twenties has a deep commitment to his buddies in the corps first, and then to his country. When you boil it down to its base, younger soldiers fight for the buddies beside them. And that's a cruel motivation.

If, on the other hand, you take a forty-year-old man who has a wife, children, property, a bank account back home, and a financial and emotional stake in his country, that's a different story. He has experienced life and freedom in the United States for twenty years as an adult. So what you have is an extremely deadly and completely untapped resource. Realistically (and unfortunately), according to today's military standards, thirty- and forty-year-old recruits aren't deemed battle ready. In addition, the country, the press, and the politicians would not tolerate the 30 percent casualty rate of all-out war it would take to get down to the older dudes. Yet our soldiers and our men know that this is a job that needs to be done and that it doesn't matter in the end how brutal and barbaric it's going to get. Brutality and barbarism is what it's going to take to win any war in the Middle East. No matter how bad it gets over there, nobody is going to come over here and fight us. And it's not because we have two oceans that border us, it's because Americans as a people bear arms.

Regarding the Iraq War, with the politicians in charge, we'll continue fighting with one hand tied behind our backs. But that can't last forever. Al-Qaeda doesn't know it yet, but someday when they finally infuriate us to the point where we pull that other arm from behind our back, with guns blazing—and with no rules of engagement, no mercy, and no quarter—they're finished. My Special Forces friend would call our retaliation "laying hate." We would exterminate them.

Until the day comes when we fully commit to fighting a real war, I'm reluctantly considering joining the camp that says, "Screw 'em, let's get out." Since this book is supposed to be about expressing opinions by drawing from my past, here's a life experience analogy to the situation in the Middle East that you might find interesting.

I was in rehab with guys who had been in treatment five or six times. They were a lost and pathetic bunch, completely forsaken by their friends. Their families would have nothing more to do with them. The only reason they were there was that the court ordered them to rehab. They had absolutely nothing left to gain or lose, because nobody would have anything to do with them whatsoever anyway.

I felt really sorry for these guys. I felt bad for them and the families who had abandoned them. How can a man get to the point where his own parents finally have to turn their backs on their own child and say, "I'm not going to help you any longer"? I've been through my fair share of testing the will and patience of my family and friends, but, thank God, they never gave up on me. I finally asked one of the counselors about it. I felt pity for these guys who had nothing. No clothes. No money. No job. No family.

"Some people never get it," the counselor told me. "For whatever reason, some people never see the light. They never have the epiphany where they finally figure out that they have to stop. They've never said to themselves, 'I'm done, I'm finished.'"

That's what these counselors had to tell these people's families: His welfare and well-being are no longer your concern. You've done everything you can do. You have to let it go and not feel guilty about it. You have to start worrying about yourself and the rest of your family. He's hopeless until he's decided to help himself. Otherwise, you're going down with him as an enabler.

This brings me to the Sunnis and Shiites in Iraq, who persist in holding on to the same grudges they've had for hundreds of years. Essentially, we've put Iraq in social and political rehab. We killed Saddam and his bloodthirsty sons and tried to show the Iraqis a better way and help them out. We've tried for five arduous years to bring them into the twenty-first century, except they absolutely refuse to come. They refuse to "get it." It's sad and heartbreaking to watch. So maybe we, as a civilized society, as guilt-ridden as we are, need to step back and absolve ourselves of the problem. Maybe we're done trying to keep the Iraq militants from killing each other. The flowers they threw at us during the first Gulf War have turned into bombs. You know what? Maybe it can't be done, and they aren't ready for a freer social order. Maybe they haven't hit rock bottom yet, so we might have to absolve ourselves of responsibility for whether or not they can coexist peacefully.

Maybe the Iraq situation is hopeless, and not because we don't have the ability to get the job done, but because we have to admit that the people we are trying to help ultimately don't want to help themselves. Maybe the situation is futile and sadly we must go home because our presence as peacekeepers is as much of a liability there as if we were the occupiers. It's a tragic but entirely possible conclusion.

What would happen if tomorrow, all of the people in the Middle East decided to throw their weapons into the sea? What would the United States as a country do? We would rejoice. How can we help?

Then ask yourself, what would Al-Qaeda do if tomorrow the United States of America threw all of its weapons into the oceans? They'd probably come over and kill us. Once again, that's the difference between us and them. If *they* laid down their weapons, we'd be there to help, whereas if they were to suddenly find *us* completely defenseless, there would be full-scale jihad.

I see two possible scenarios when it comes to our foreign policy in the Middle East. Both deal with a concept I call Orkinism.

Scenario 1: Originally the majority of Iraqis were appreciative of us liberating them from Saddam. But the situation soon got out of hand. It was like they had a huge cockroach problem in their house, so the Orkin guy came over and killed all the cockroaches. But then he moved into the house! Now he's eating their food, drinking their beer, and making love to their wife. He was even seen spanking one of their kids! Maybe all the Iraqis want is for the Orkin man to do his job and then leave and go home.

Scenario 2: Some Iraqis live in a huge apartment building. After the Orkin man kills the cockroaches in their apartment, more cockroaches keep coming from everybody else's apartments. So maybe the Orkin man needs to stay because the other tenants in the building won't let him in to kill *their* cockroaches. Maybe the whole building needs to band together and hire a live-in exterminator because not everybody in the building is killing their cockroaches. It's a dirty job, but somebody has to do it.

Chapter Thirty-one

ARLINGTON

I T WAS THE FIRST TIME SCOTT HENDRICKS EVER PHONED about a song. I was out at my farm.

"Trace, you need to come downtown and hear this song."

"I'm coming in tomorrow."

"No. You need to come downtown right now and hear this song."

Hmm. So I jumped in my truck, drove downtown, and walked into his office.

"All right, here I am, and this better be good."

Then he played me a demo of "Arlington." Man, it hit me. Whoa! I immediately knew I would record it. After we cut it, we decided to make it one of our videos.

Shooting the video for "Arlington" was a powerful experience. Usually when we make a video we shoot the same scenes again and again and again. Then we reposition the camera and change the lighting and shoot it again. But when we filmed at Arlington, with me laying the wreath at the Tomb of the Unknown Soldier, we had one try, and that was it. I don't know who made that happen, but I was in total awe being next to those honor guards. The solemn pomp of the Arlington ceremony is a thing of beauty, like standing at the top of those concrete stairs and walking down those steps with the honor guard by my side.

When we brought our cameras to Arlington I told the director that the scene we shot at the tomb needed to be low-key and discreet. There were funerals going on that day, and visitors and tourists standing around. I didn't want anybody to know we were filming. The crew did it mostly with handheld cameras, and maybe one mounted camera. It was very subtle. We didn't want to disrupt what was going on out there. We got our shots and went about our business.

Arlington National Cemetery is 624 acres of land across the Potomac River from Washington, D.C. It became a military cemetery during the Civil War and was originally an estate called Arlington House, which was owned by the family of Mary Anna Custis Lee, Robert E. Lee's wife. General Lee lived there, and after the Civil War, the Union powers converted the land into a graveyard. It was originally done to spite General Lee so he would never be able to live in that house again. But transforming the estate into a military cemetery became an honor in the long run.

The main scenes where I'm walking through the graveyard were not filmed at Arlington. We shot those at another nearby military cemetery. The reason we chose an alternate locale was because that particular cemetery's grave sites were all taken, and so there were no ceremonies going on.

It was a moving experience to walk around Arlington Cemetery. It's such a holy place. I got to stand at the grave of the young soldier, Corporal Patrick Ray Nixon, who was the inspiration for the song.

Dave Turnbull, one of the writers of "Arlington," got the idea for the song after his mother came to Nashville to visit him. As I heard the story, she and Dave went out to purchase a new car.

They went down to the dealership, and Dave's mother started making small talk with the salesman. When he asked her where she was from, she told him she was from Virginia.

"I just got back from Virginia to visit my son," the salesman told her. "He's in Arlington."

"Oh yes," she said, "Arlington is a nice area."

"Actually," he said, "we buried my son in Arlington Cemetery."

The salesman, David Nixon, related the whole story to Turnbull. David Nixon was in the Marine Corps and served in Vietnam. His son Patrick joined the Marines and was sent to Iraq, where he was killed. David explained what an honor it was to have his son lying in Arlington. Here was a man whose son made it to the most sacred and honorable place any soldier could. Dave hooked up with Jeremy Spillman and told him the story and they wrote the song together.

After we cut the tune and finished it, I phoned David Nixon. I had never met him.

"Look, I want you to come and hear this song. It was inspired by your son. But I need you to hear it first. Since it's your story, I want your blessing and approval. If you don't like it, nobody will ever hear it."

So David Nixon and his wife and daughter came down to Scott Hendricks's office with me, Scott, and the songwriters. When we played the song, everybody in the room cried. I wept because it was overpowering seeing what that song meant to a proud father. David has remained my friend, and we stay in contact. Although I play "Arlington" at nearly every concert, it was well worth recording just for the opportunity to play it for David and his family.

Sometimes a song packs emotional punch depending on where you sing it. "Arlington" is a very special song on my set list, but it has never been more special than when I performed it on the deck of the USS *Intrepid* in New York City at a Veterans Day salute in 2006. I was up on deck with all these decorated military guys who had actually served at sea on the famous aircraft carrier. They brought all the older veterans back for the ceremony. So I got up and sang "Arlington," and, boy, it was hard. I looked out there and saw these men with tears in their eyes, and it was brutal. I was sure that every one of those guys had friends in Arlington, or a loved one resting in a military cemetery somewhere else. The one thing about that song is that I wish it had been written to encompass *all* of our national burial grounds, not just Arlington. There are so many across the nation and they're all hallowed ground.

I have families come to me before my show, at meet-and-greets, bringing pictures of their sons who have been killed in action in Iraq or wherever, telling me how much that song means to them. When I sing "Arlington," sometimes they're sitting in the front rows where I can see them, and although it's hard to get through the song, I'll sing it just for them, and I'll get through it pretty good. It's all I can do to show my appreciation and help them handle their grief.

I SEE A LOT of America from my seat on the bus. When I tour, I see the whole economic landscape. We'll drive through the affluent areas. Then we go into the next zip code and it's depressed. I can see the subtle difference between one town and the next, but I can never figure out why one little town is clean and well-kept while the next town is trashy and run down. I see a lot more towns like that lately. Lots of places have degenerated into dirty little towns. I don't understand that. Some people give up on their towns. They don't care anymore. No civic pride of ownership.

In the last decade, my own hometown has tried to make a comeback. I remember when all the little stores on Main Street were boarded up. For a while there, Sarepta really looked dilapidated. The whole town looked like it needed a pressure wash and a coat of paint. I'd like to see that change for the better in the next several years.

I've got a front-row seat to America from the window of my bus. I meet people. I talk to folks. I hang out. I can see the patriotism that's out there, and believe me, it's out there. But at the same time, there's a frustration with our leaders in Washington. All these people in Small Town, U.S.A., feel like they've been forgotten. Their towns have gone to seed. Their portion of the economy has gone to hell. Yes, they support our troops and the conservative agenda, but at the same time, enough already. Nothing's getting done. The frustration is off the chart. When a political party has been in power and controlled the executive branch, the legislative branch, both houses of Congress, and now the Supreme Court, and you *still* can't get anything done, then you're totally inept. And that's the way most blue-collar, hardworking guys and gals look at America. We don't understand it. If you've supposedly got people of like mind running the show, and you *still* can't get anything done, then evidently our leaders don't have any balls.

We are a compassionate, caring country. We'll spend a million dollars looking for three knotheads who climbed a snowcapped mountain and got lost one weekend. Or a couple of lost, mentally challenged whales in California. Other countries might think, mountain climbers and whales, screw 'em. Not us. By God, we'll spend millions of dollars and devote manpower and helicopters and dogs and call out the Coast Guard. Coverage on every network news channel.

Yet where is the compassion for the average working men and women who lay down their lives so that we can live free?

What is it going to take to make this country great, for our leaders to find the courage to ask us all to sacrifice? Unlike the soldiers buried in Arlington, we haven't been asked to sacrifice one bit. Republicans view sacrifice as a weakness; Democrats see it as guilt. They want us to think that everything is under control. We want to live in our nice homes and have all the luxuries. We want to drive our flashy automobiles and enjoy a government that runs like a well-oiled machine. And we want everybody in the world to leave us alone. As far as I can see, the only people who are truly sacrificing are the troops overseas and their families. So, shame on the rest of us.

When is the government going to realize that the American people need to be asked—or forced—to sacrifice? Sadly, not until we get to the point that our very survival is threatened. That's when we'll all get with the program. Only then will it happen. We'll finally come together as a people, play for the same team, and do what needs to be done. Until then, there will always be constant bickering, with special interests first, and America second.

Chapter Thirty-two

NASHVILLE BADONKADONK

U NFORTUNATELY, I DON'T WRITE ENOUGH SONGS THESE days. At the risk of talking about myself in the third person and sounding like I've lost my mind, Career Trace killed off Creative Trace. Writing with a co-writer is the way most people in country compose today, and that's the way I like to write (although it seems like we're seeing more threesomes writing than we used to). It's a lot of fun writing with other people. I enjoy the creative input and throwing ideas around. You might have a concept for a song and take it one way, then with somebody else's input it goes someplace completely different, and a lot of times it's for the better.

Nashville is full of the best songwriters in the world and I sure am lucky that I know a lot of them. They're everywhere and they practice their craft every day because it's their full-time gig. I've gotten to a point in my career where songwriters will get together and collaborate on a tune, and as soon as they finish the song, they'll look at each other and say, "Damn. That sounds like a Trace song. Let's just send it over to him."

Because of the sexy stuff that I've recorded over the years, some songwriters will write a tune that they think is incredibly nasty and that nobody else would ever record, and they send it to me because they know I'm probably the only shot they have. Some of the stuff I get is so raunchy, even I won't sing it. I get some nasty, nasty stuff.

I know a lot of artists, but personally, I'm not comfortable with the term *artist*. Vincent van Gogh. Pablo Picasso. Beethoven. Ray Charles. Those guys were artists. Me? I sing and do the "dick dance." There's no art to that. The real artists in the music industry are the ones who play their instruments, write their own songs, and sing their tunes. If you can do all three of those things, then, in my opinion, congratulations, you are an artist. When I think of artists, I think of Bob Dylan or James Taylor or Keith Urban—guys who are amazing musicians, good singers, and imaginative songwriters. Keith does all those things. The same goes for Vince Gill and Brad Paisley—those guys are what I define as artists.

I know a lot of artists who listen to music all the time, and I'm jealous of those guys. I'm envious because I wish I could. Music for me is an everyday job. It's the life I live, which can result in overload. I look at it this way: I doubt if there are many plumbers who, at the end of a long day, go home and crawl up under the sink in their kitchen and take the trap off just for the sheer fun of it. That's kind of the way I am with music. I'm so busy and have been on the road so much during the last few years, that once I get home, I don't listen to much music.

I'm a decent songwriter. I've written some hits. I feel guilty that I'm not writing because I'm not doing all I can do to provide for my children on the publishing side. Maybe I could be more like Bill Anderson and pick up a head of creative steam and write a whole bunch of songs. I should block out time just to write, but so far I haven't done that. As my year gets booked up with touring and obligations, it seems as if my life is scheduled nonstop. By the end of the year, I take a long break from Thanksgiving until the second or third week of January. When I see that break coming I can't wait to get there and hang out at my farm.

Although I belong to the Grand Ole Opry and sit on the Country Music Association board, I don't really hang out that much with other country stars. Over the past ten years that I've been in the community, I've never had a close enough relationship with many folks in music that I could truly hang out with them. It's as if everybody's going in different directions, doing their own thing, and working on their careers so hard that nobody has the time to forge close friendships.

The other day I was speaking with my old runnin' buddy, Todd Burns (one of my pre-record-deal friends that I try to stay in touch with), about how we both have been guilty of sacrificing friends for careers. In fact, I don't have that many friends that I don't have on the payroll. It's gotten to the point where I don't have the time. It's not because I want it that way. It is how it is. Just when you think things are going to slow down, when you're no longer the hamster in the wheel, life speeds up again. Until you decide to hang up your spurs and just quit, you're always going to try to remain a viable commodity, and in this business, that means working, working, and more working.

I fulfilled my original contract with Capitol Nashville when I released *Dangerous Man,* my seventh album. That's a rarity in any music genre. It's highly unusual for an artist to actually finish out their contract, so I'm proud of that. Capitol's been good to me. The regime that is there now is very supportive. They seem to be into what I do, so why should I go anywhere else? So I signed up for five more albums.

—

IT'S NOT EASY these days to sell a million copies of a record. It's all about the one song that connects with the people. Usually, you never know which one it will be. "Honky Tonk Badonkadonk" was that song for me.

The first time I heard "Honky Tonk Badonkadonk," Scott Hendricks played it for me. One of the co-writers, Jamey Johnson, sang it on a smokin' demo. When Scott played it for me in his office, I laughed out loud. I got the joke immediately.

"That's freakin' funny! I've gotta cut that tune!"

It was a simple as that. I talked to Jamey Johnson and Randy Houser, and they told me how they wrote the song. Apparently they were in Nashville's Wild Horse Saloon one night watching this girl with a big ass knocking people off the dance floor. She was really working it. Then either Jamey or Randy, I don't know which, said, "Look at the badonkadonk on that one."

The other guy said, "Honky-tonk badonkadonk." They wrote the song the very next day. Jamey told me it didn't take them very long to finish it.

Even though it might be my most famous song, technically "Badonkadonk" was never a number-one record, and for pretty good reason. It was number two the same week Carrie Underwood went number one with "Jesus, Take the Wheel." Right behind me, at number three, was Brad Paisley's "When I Get Where I'm Going," a song about heaven. So there I was, in a sticky position. I couldn't exactly root against the records ahead of or behind me. I couldn't pray to the man upstairs, asking, "Lord, could you please make my 'ass' record number one instead of the two 'Jesus' songs?" It would have been wrong. And that's probably why it didn't go number one. I had ass, they had Jesus, and Jesus won, which I guess is the way it ought to be.

We knew that "Badonkadonk" was going to be as polarizing as it was successful. We knew people would either love it or hate it, and there wasn't going to be any middle ground. The hip-hop and rap angle was also extremely controversial. Then there was also the so-called denigration of women. I guess you can call it exploitative, but I call it appreciative. It's just two different ways of looking at the same end (pardon the pun).

Still, I was lucky to get the song. Songs get taken on a first come, first served basis. That's how it's *supposed* to work, but it doesn't always go that way. I've had bigger acts cut songs I've had on hold. If you put a song on hold and some bigger act wants it, and if the publisher sees dollar signs, they'll grant the license to the bigger act. It just so happened I got to play the part of the big dog on "Badonkadonk."

The same thing happens with hiring band members. As soon as you get your touring band super tight, some bigger fish above you looks down and says, "Man, that's a good band, and I like that guy right there."

The next thing you know, he's playing with that guy. It's happened to me, and I've done it to other guys as well. An act might be opening a show, and the next thing they know, their guitar player is playing with the headliner. In this business, we cannibalize ourselves. We eat our young. We eat our old. We eat each other. The music business is incestuous and cannibalistic and just plain hungry!

Nashville is both a huge network and a small clique. I don't know if the clique is as important to me as it should be, but to some people it is *very* important. Some folks operate and survive by being part of the clique. Me, since I don't socialize that much, I just do my thing and let the others do their power networking. I'm generally not down at the Longhorn having lunch at the see-and-be-seen restaurant where all the Music Row movers and shakers go. Instead, I'm probably driving to the farm, enjoying a SuperSonic burger with cheese and jalapeños and what little time I have to myself.

I've learned through the years that in order to sell records, you have to create passion. Passion is good, whether it's one way or the other. If you create passion where somebody either loves or hates something, it'll sell. So if you put out a record and half the listening audience hates it, but the other half loves it, I'll take that any day over a record that everybody thinks is "kinda sorta pretty good." I don't want kinda sorta. Give me a half-hatin', half-lovin' record and I'll show you some passion. The bottom line, in order for me to keep *making* records, I have to *sell* records. And that's how you sell records, by stirring up the passion.

Chapter Thirty-three

A GLASS-HALF-EMPTY GUY

EVERYBODY HAS THEIR STAGE "LOOK." MINE HAS changed a little over the years, but the constants have always been ponytail, custom-made Wrangler jeans, and of course the hat. I've worn a cowboy hat for a long time, but these days I don't wear it that much in public. Nowadays I stick my ponytail up under my baseball cap, put on a pair of sunglasses, and go anywhere I want to go in relative anonymity. Only now and then will anybody recognize me. Even then, they're not sure. But the second I drop that tail down and put that cowboy hat on, it's over. It's a shame that I can't wear a hat anymore. But hell, it's a good trade-off. If that's all I have to give up to enjoy the finer things in life, then maybe that's okay.

But still, the hat hits on a deeper thing. In giving up my cowboy hat, have I also given up my principles and sacrificed my character? Is anything—money or fame—worth *that*? I don't know. Maybe I'll write another book twenty years from now and see if I can still tolerate myself. Let's see if I'm proud of whatever legacy I left behind.

I'm a glass-half-empty guy. That's just how I am. A pessimist. I tend to look on the dark side, and I always prepare for the worst-case scenario. What is the worst possible outcome? That's how I look at every situation. That way, if things don't work out perfectly, at least it's not as bad as it could have been.

When I see those happy, giddy people who run around feeling jovial, smiling, laughing, and giggling . . . man, those people get on my nerves. They must be going through life with blissful blinders on. Can't you see what the hell is going on around here? What are you so freaking happy about? Everything is *not* cool. Live in the real world with the rest of us. How dare you be so happy all the time?

I like the hits I've had, but most of my favorite songs are the darker album tracks. Songs like "She's Still There," "Someday," "Out of My Dreams," "Welcome to Hell," and "Every Other Friday at Five." They're usually too dark for radio play, but those are my favorites. When I finish a record and I listen through it, I have the same reaction every time: I could have done that better. I should have sung a different lick right there. Usually, my songs start to really come to life after I've been singing them live for about a year. If it were totally left up to me, I would probably record such a morbid album that you would have to hide the knives and guns to listen to it.

I once did a program for the Great American Country cable channel. They came out to the farm and we sat down and did an in-depth interview. After they edited it, I looked like the most depressed SOB on earth. The interviewer, Lorianne, asked me if I was happy.

Happy? Happy is an emotion that comes and goes. My problem is that I obsess over things too much to be happy, but that's the addict in me. I'm a perfectionist, another reason why I say I'm not a fan of me. I don't think of happiness as a state of being. That's not how I perceive happiness. Happiness is something that comes in waves. It's like sex. It's great, but it only lasts for a little while. Then you have to get back in your coffin that's lined with broken glass.

Is that dark enough for you?

Chapter Thirty-four

SINGIN' AND PLAYIN' FOR THE PEOPLE

FIGURE THAT EVERY TIME SOMEBODY COMES TO MY SHOW and buys a ticket, he's voting for me with his wallet. That poor bastard probably worked half a day to earn the money to come to my show, and if he took his old lady, that's a whole day's pay.

He voted for me.

I've spent three years and counting serving on the board of the Country Music Association. Nashville's Music Row has a tight relationship with all of the top industry organizations, including the CMA, the Academy of Country Music (which gave me a Top New Vocalist award), and the National Academy of Recording Arts and Sciences (NARAS), the folks who hand out the Grammy Awards.

I joined the CMA to learn the inner workings of the music business, especially the world of country music.

The one thing the members of NARAS, CMA, and the Academy need to remember is that country music is for the fans, first and foremost. It's not about us! It's about them! I don't make records to impress my peers. I make records hoping that the person driving his or her truck down the turnpike will buy it. It's for them, and that's all it's for.

At first I was shocked when the Dixie Chicks won five Grammys in 2007. Then I thought, Wait a minute, this was political, man. This was the East Coast and West Coast entertainment establishment sticking their thumbs in the eyes of true country fans, many of whom live in the Midwest. That's all it was. Politics as usual. The Grammy voters sent their antiwar, anti-Bush message to all the red-state people who live in Flyover Land, the small cities and towns these people fly over in their private jets on their way back and forth between New York and Los Angeles. It made the Grammy Awards look unsympathetic to the average working people who listen to country music.

Country fans must have scratched their heads in confusion when the Dixie Chicks swept the Grammys that night. They weren't representative of today's country music: The Dixie Chicks aren't played on country radio anymore. In my opinion, Natalie Maines behaved badly when she uttered those words onstage in England about Bush and Texas. She didn't stand up and say she was sorry. I'm not saying she should be sorry for *what* she said. It's *how* and *where* she said it.

Like I say in one of my songs, "Don't say nothin' you can't take back."

Maines could have said, "Look, I should have expressed my frustration and disappointment in another way. I shouldn't have said it *when* I said it and *where* I said it. I could have worded it better, and I shouldn't have said it onstage in a foreign country."

If she would have apologized and admitted her mistake, country music fans would have let the Chicks back into the fold. But she won't do it, so the band has lost credibility with the millions who bought their earlier CDs. (Luckily for them, they don't care.)

After watching the 2007 Grammy Awards on television (and switching back and forth between that and an Ultimate Fighting match on Showtime), I had this epiphany: I could put together a better country awards show that would only last an hour. Let the artists sing their own songs and showcase some of our people who have done well that year—and that means honoring those who sold the most concert tickets and records and add a couple of newcomers we think will be hot further down the road. That's the whole show, and during the program we would present an award for whoever sold the most tickets that year.

"Ladies and gentleman, Rascal Flatts!"

Then Rascal Flatts comes out and gets their doorstop, waves, and goes home.

"One more award for the most records sold!"

"Ladies and gentleman, Kenny Chesney!"

Then Kenny comes out and picks up his doorstop or boat anchor or whatever you want to call it and the show is over.

The People's Choice Awards are important to me because the fans vote! I was truly shocked at how many of them voted for me this year. I was nominated for a 2007 People's Choice Award along with Kenny Chesney and Toby Keith. Another cool thing about the People's Choice music categories is that country artists are integrated with the other pop music formats, not segregated. For example, for the Favorite Male Singer category, which Kenny won, all three nominees were country! And it was actual fans voting, not the elitist music industry gatekeepers who decide politically on the winners. Unless the votes are skewed or distorted in some way that I don't know about, bravo to the People's Choice Awards for letting the music consumers choose the winners. They're the ones putting their money on the counter, so that's the way it should be.

The most ironic part of this whole awards fracas is that, to a lot of country artists, the Grammy is highly desirable because it seems to be the hardest one to win. But in my opinion, the NARAS voters are generally uninformed about modern country. They care more about retro acts or some pop crossover country act than they do mainstream country artists.

I think the only people who should be allowed to vote on who makes the best music are the folks who *pay* for it. Not the people who steal it off the Internet. Not the people who illegally download it. Not the people who get it sent to them for free in a cute little box from the record labels saying, "Please listen and vote for us, and here's your free copy." The people who buy their CDs should be the ones allowed to vote and determine the winners.

Here's how all this relates to the big picture.

California has got this whole country completely screwed up. It has a tremendous left-wing, radically liberal say in how things get done in our country. California is the cultural center of bleeding-heart guilt. Since California and New York have the most representatives in the House, and they happen to frequently elect liberal Democrats, they run things. California is opposed to nuclear power, so we all pay way too much for energy. Both coasts dictate how our country is run while the rest of us stuck in the middle are truly stuck, dictated to by the people who fly over our heads. The New York melting pot combined with the Los Angeles everything-goes attitude means the people stuck in the middle are getting squeezed with no voice, no vote, and no say in how this country is being run. And don't even get me started on San Francisco. Honestly, I think most of the people in the South and the Midwest have pretty much written off California. They feel that somewhere along the way, we lost California. It's as if it's no longer a part of our nation. The Californians do their own thing. They have their own codes and standards as they tell the rest of us what scumbag hicks we are and that we're not enlightened enough. I take strong exception to that.

Some celebrities believe they are better informed about what's going on. That's why actors, actresses, and singers speak out about politics so much these days. They think they're more knowledgeable than the people who work regular nine-to-five jobs.

I'll let you in on a secret: Those Hollywood–New York people are no more intelligent and enlightened than you are. Do your own research and do your legwork and vote how your heart tells you to vote. Don't be swayed by anything anybody famous might have to say, especially entertainers, because they've bought into their own hype in thinking that because they are artists, they are somehow connected in a deeper, more spiritual way than you are. They've bought into their own bullshit.

And for God's sake, don't go into the booth and pull the curtain and pull a lever because you heard me or Natalie Maines or Bruce Springsteen or any celebrity say that they support a certain candidate or cause. Learn all you can and think for yourself.

To me, the award show shortcomings are akin to what's screwed up about this nation. Politicians are elected to go to Washington, D.C., to serve at the will of the people and do what *we* want them to do, not what *they* want to do. It's not about patting each other on the back behind closed doors and talking about how smart they are and what a good job they're doing. Washington (and Nashville) has to make sure it's representing the real constituency and not just a bunch of special interests.

The larger point here is that as a country, we've become deeply fragmented. And it's only getting worse. With scorched-earth political tactics and a lack of compromise and cooperation among lawmakers, that special-interest, me-first mind-set spreads to the voters. As our nation becomes more polarized, we like-minded people will just talk (and blog) amongst ourselves. Pretty soon there won't be any unity in this country. Just flocks of self-interested sheep.

The politicians in Washington have demonstrated a lack of will to do anything about the problems that the American people are screaming about—like corrupt government officials who lie and steal, winning the war in Iraq, and controlling illegal immigration. While we're screaming at them to do something, they refuse to take a stand until it becomes do-or-die. And when they finally do something, it'll be the wrong thing. Meanwhile, we'll just sit out here together and get all pissed off and frustrated and gripe about how unfair it all is. About how this nation is run by people totally disconnected from reality.

Just like the Grammys.

Chapter Thirty-five

MORE MORAL AND LESS CIVIL

DON'T THINK THE AVERAGE BUBBA LOOKS AT BILL CLINTON as your typical Southern good ol' boy. While people outside the South might relate to Bill Clinton as a Bubba, I *certainly* don't think of him as one. I view him more as somebody who was corrupted by power and the political system. Maybe he used to be a country boy a long time ago, but I don't think he was when he started out in politics. He was a nerd. He was in the school band. He was a Rhodes scholar. He wanted to be the next John F. Kennedy.

Political folks say Bill Clinton's presidency stood for economic prosperity just like Ronald Reagan's. In my opinion, history will judge his presidency differently. True, lots of dot-com folks got rich on his watch, but it's also been proven that he dropped the ball on key problems we now have to face. I believe that because of his presidency, all the Islamic terrorist chickens are now coming home to roost because of what he didn't do. I also believe that he had several opportunities to eliminate bin Laden and key Al-Qaeda operatives. He denies he missed opportunities to kill bin Laden. Remember when he yelled at Chris Wallace on national television? It's been strongly suggested, by people who know, that President Clinton had several good chances to eliminate bin

Laden when the terrorist lived in a house in Yemen and Bill didn't do it.

I still can't forget that shameful military incident when the bodies of American soldiers were dragged through the streets of Somalia. If that had happened on President Ronald Reagan or President George W.'s watch instead of Clinton's, the commander in chief would have leveled that place. The American military should have waxed ass. But Clinton did nothing. When Al-Qaeda blew a hole in the side of the USS *Cole* so big you could have driven my tour bus through it, President Clinton didn't do a damn thing about it. Somebody should have died over that bombing, including bin Laden. Harvard and Yale's favorite Bubba didn't do squat. He may have been civil, but he wasn't moral.

We assess and judge people today in terms of civility rather than morality. One hundred and fifty years ago, people strived to be both moral and civil. Then the times shifted. Today, morality is secondary as long as you're civil, and we have this attitude that it's none of our business what some people do in private as long as they're civil in public.

I understand how morality can be a moving target with the times. Yet we look back and try to discredit men in history like Thomas Jefferson or Nathan Bedford Forrest, which isn't quite fair. You can't judge a nineteenth-century man by twenty-first-century societal standards. So if Forrest sold slaves and Jefferson owned them in the nineteenth century, it's difficult to smugly justify or condemn them by today's standards. Unfortunately, only a minority of people back then were moral enough (by today's standards) to realize that slavery was wrong, while a large majority were civil about it. Times were different. There were customs and social mores that were acceptable then that certainly aren't now, and vice versa. But the door swings both ways. Just as we don't want to be judged by *yesterday's* standards, let's not judge great men and their deeds by *today's* standards of morality and civility.

If you look at Bill Clinton and George W. Bush, our forty-second and forty-third presidents, Clinton might be considered very civil but somewhat immoral, while Bush is considered very moral and, in certain ways, uncivil. My perceived difference between liberalism and conservatism is this: Liberalism seems less moral, yet civil, while conservatism is more moral and less civil.

Take, for example, the portrait of a do-gooder: someone who appears to contribute selflessly to the world. Motivation for performing community service and charity work differs radically between *genuine* conservatives and liberals. I'm talking about people who, at their core, are either truly conservative- or truly liberal-minded. I believe that liberals take on causes in order to make themselves feel better about themselves while conservatives do things simply to help other folks out. Me, I try to be anonymous when it comes to charity work. I'll lend my time to children's causes because children are truly the innocent ones and they don't deserve any of the bad breaks that befall them.

THESE DAYS I *have* to lean more toward the Republican Party because they're *supposed* to be the conservatives. Many of them are not, but since I consider myself a conservative, for now it's the only place for me to go. Until a viable third party emerges, I'm a Republican because I've picked the lesser of two evils.

I've been invited at least three times to appear at major Republican campaign stops during 2003. Vice President Dick Cheney's office has invited me to attend some of his shindigs, but I don't know, man. I just couldn't go. I'm a conservative, but I'm just like all the other conservatives in this country in that I'm so incredibly frustrated with the Republican Party at this point. I just couldn't get down with the program. I just couldn't throw my lot in with them last time around.

Although I didn't attend the Republican convention in 2004, I did do a show at a club in New York after the delegates nominated Bush to run for his second term. We played this weird club that once was a church, before they turned it into a nightclub. It was a bizarre night. There were a bunch of drunken suits in the audience. Congressman Dennis Hastert (not drunk) spoke before we started playing. It was a strange billing that didn't make any sense whatsoever. There was me, Isaac Hayes, and Kid Rock.

I went out and played about thirty minutes. I picked out the most rockin' stuff I had, a half hour of balls-out music. Isaac Hayes did "Shaft" and all that cool R&B stuff. Then Kid Rock walked out onstage and grabbed the microphone and screamed, "ARE YOU MOTHERF**KERS SCARED?"

I couldn't believe it. I smiled a wide grin. All right! I didn't really know what he meant, but I think he appreciated the weirdness, too. It was a surreal moment.

I've met my fair share of professional athletes, military men, political dignitaries and government VIPs throughout my career. I once sang at a function in Washington, D.C., and President G. H. W. Bush, was there. I got to joke with him after we took a picture together. I asked him where Mrs. Bush was.

"People ask me that all the time," he said. "That's all they want to know. Where's Barbara? Where's Barbara? Doesn't anybody want to talk to me?" He was joking, but I apologized anyway. Once I got onstage, I relayed the story and got a big laugh. "So, please allow me to beg your forgiveness," I said to the former president from the stage, "but I'm going to have to sing this next song for Barbara. I was really wantin' to see *her*, and all I got was you."

I figured that afterward, he went back and told her what I had said. I guess he dug it because a few weeks later Barbara Bush wrote me a personal, handwritten thank-you note.

Chapter Thirty-six

THE "I'M COOL" CARD

LIKE IT OR NOT, WE ALL HAVE TO DEAL WITH AIRPORT security whenever we fly. At least the 299 million of us who don't own our own planes do. One day after a gig in Fort Lauderdale, Florida, I wanted to fly back to Nashville instead of riding home on the bus. But I left my ID in my truck in Tennessee. I literally needed a police escort to the airport and a special security clearance to board the plane. It was a pretty big ordeal.

This got me to thinking, Why can't we have the I'm Cool Card? Don't leave home without it!

Just whip your card out at airport security and it says I'm Cool. I don't know exactly how you'd do it. An intense background check and probably some psychoanalysis might be involved, but because of our jobs, there are people like me who would be willing to go through all the flaming hoops and hurdles in order to get the I'm Cool Card. Then we could have a separate I'm Cool Card line at the airport where you could just walk through and flash your I'm Cool Card and head to the plane. It's not a matter of being elitist, just separating the wheat from the chaff, the constant from the casual traveler.

I know people will get all freaked out about the Big Brother thing. Look, if you're not doing anything wrong, then Big

Brother *shouldn't* bother you. So, do a background check on me. I don't care. Maybe I wouldn't qualify for the I'm Cool Card, but I'd like to have a shot at it. Maybe Homeland Security can combine it with the instant thumbprint or the retina scan to eliminate forgery.

I think the I'm Cool Card is an idea whose time has come, but they'll probably screw it up somehow. Somebody will complain that it's profiling or that it's discriminatory in some way. I can already see that coming. The ACLU will say, "Well, not everybody can get it." So we'll continue to stand in those lines, and get prodded along like cattle.

Another thing about the airline industry that infuriates me is the way baggage handlers go out of their way to destroy your luggage. Do you remember a Samsonite commercial several years ago that showed a chimp abusing a piece of their luggage? I believe they wanted to use one of the actual "gorillas" employed by the airline industry, their union said, "Absolutely not!"

I'm serious, though. Watch them load the plane the next time you fly, and notice the extra effort it takes to lift the bag a few feet higher than is necessary in order to slam it on the conveyor belt. I bet they sit in the break room and brag to each other about how many people's personal belongings they've destroyed since lunch

I was on an airplane recently and saw the pilot walk out of the cockpit during the flight to take a leak. He had his sidearm right on his belt. I thought, all right, this flight is safe. Flying rednecks!

If I was a commercial airline pilot, hell yeah, I'd be armed— whether the FAA let me do it or not. If you want me to fly that plane, I'm gonna be packin' heat.

So when you fly, do you try to pick out who the air marshal is? Sometimes you can spot them. I keep reading about how some passengers freak out and go into air rage and have to be restrained by the other passengers onboard. Wow! None of that cool shit ever happens when I fly. But if it did, I would, in my most Southern genteel way, offer my services.

"May I subdue the idiot? Please allow me."

Chapter Thirty-seven

BUBBA BYTES: NEWS AND VIEWS FROM A ROUGHNECK COUNTRY BOY

WHEN I WAS FIRST STARTING OUT IN THE MUSIC business, a contract would come in and I'd skip over all the stuff on top and get to that line at the bottom that tells how much they're paying. And I'd say, "Yeah, okay, we'll do that one." You show up at the gig first and ask questions later.

Once I played a club, I think in Tucson, a honky-tonk that was a multipurpose kind of room. Every night of the week, they catered to a different audience. During the sound check I went over to shoot some pool, and there were pictures on the wall of guys shooting stick without their shirts on. It seemed odd to me. I ignored it but later on I found out that one night a week the place was a gay club.

Now the gay rights movement doesn't freak me out too much. But don't ask me if I've seen *Brokeback Mountain,* because I don't intend to ever see it. Actually, I'm a little tired of the whole subject. You have extremists screaming on each end of every debate, on both the left and right. The same is true with the gay marriage question. The extreme view on the pro side of the gay marriage issue is that it be called marriage. I think that's going too far.

Okay, I figure I'll meet you folks more than halfway. I'm willing to support civil unions. If you enter into a civil union, you can have *all the rights* and benefits that married couples enjoy and receive. There you go: Isn't that what you wanted in the first place? Don't you want the tax benefits and the health insurance and the access to estates? Through civil unions, gay couples are welcome to *all* the legal benefits that married couples get. But please don't call it marriage, okay? I know it's just semantics, but words have meaning. And that's where I draw the line—and please don't call me homophobic, or whatever y'all call it, because I'm not afraid (or phobic), least of all of lesbians and gays. Lots of gays are country music fans.

HERE'S A BIT of sage advice. Don't say nothin' you can't take back. I read that they've expanded drug and alcohol rehab for celebrities to include sensitivity training rehab. How about Asshole Rehab? We all heard about the TV stars that used offensive slurs in public, and the drunken movie star who made anti-Semitic remarks to the cops. Haven't we all done or said something at one time or another that we regret, that we don't have any excuse for? With Asshole Rehab, we can say whatever we want to say, say it in a way that's going to make a headline, and then it's off to Asshole Rehab you go.

I AM A HUGE Dennis Miller fan and I miss seeing him on HBO. This is just one of the reasons I am a fan. He said "What is the national debt anyway? Is this money we actually owe somebody? And if it is, screw 'em. Come and get it. We ain't paying y'all. We know we've run up this huge tab, but we seem to be a little strapped for cash. We're sorry. Our bad."

That's, of course, not a direct quote, but you get the gist; and I agree wholeheartedly. I am a Dennis Miller conservative. Dennis for president!

HUGO CHÁVEZ IS the modern-day Fidel Castro socialist. He called President George Bush a sulfur-smelling devil and wants to install himself as a dictator and nationalize big industry in his native Venezuela. The clowns in the Middle East are one thing, but this dude lives in my neighborhood. He's not the bully who lives two towns over that you don't like. This son of a bitch lives on my street. What needs to happen is that all the families in the neighborhood need to unite and stick a bottle rocket up this guy's ass, light the fuse, and his attitude will change. Or . . . we could do something similar to what Reagan did to Gaddafi.

We can't allow this jerkoff to be in our Western Hemisphere neighborhood and shoot his mouth off the way he does. He's making our property values go down. He's got to clean his place up, mow his yard, and put a coat of paint on his house, and quit being such a dick. (And stop dating Danny Glover!)

Meanwhile, I will never go into a Citgo gas station ever again. I promise you, given their affiliation with Venezuela, if I ran out of gas across the street from one of their stations I would rather call a tow truck than buy a gallon of gasoline from them. At least until this guy is history.

If I was president and Hugo Chávez flew to the United Nations and insulted me like he did President George W., that bastard's plane would never have made it back to Venezuela from New York. And the same thing would apply to Mahmoud Ahmadinejad, that loudmouth president of Iran. The minute he landed on U.S. soil I would make Mahmoud our hostage. And you know what? Everybody else in the world would breathe a sigh of relief that both of them were gone.

I AM SO TIRED of hearing Karl Rove's name. I don't get the liberal venom directed toward this guy, because I don't see Rove as the Wizard of Oz the way they do. He's not the man behind the curtain. Sure, he advises the president, and I think he probably wields influence, but I don't believe guys like Rove make the final call in key matters. He might help shape the public agenda, but his political opponents give him a lot more credit than he deserves. I think the president makes the final calls himself. (Oh, shit!)

THE WAR ON terror is like herpes. People can live with it, but it'll flare up from time to time. I know this because I saw the commercial about the latest wonder drug that helps control it while watching TV with my mother. It came on right after the commercial about erectile dysfunction . . . but I digress. A lot of nations in Europe are paying the price for letting so many of these Islamic extremists into their countries. If Europe is considered an enlightened region, I don't want to be enlightened. I think Great Britain is a powderkeg. You talk about politicians that have become completely pussified. What ever happened to the stiff upper lip? Winston Churchill, despite his mistake inventing Iraq, is going to come back from the dead and kick somebody's ass for what that country's turned into.

The same is true with Canada! Supposedly Canada has the cleanest water and the best beer and a whole lot of oil. They've been sucking on our tit for so long now, and that's another thing that I would do if I was president. I would make a phone call to the Canadians and say, "Look, fellas, the only reason the Russkies didn't come over in the 1970s and kick your ass is because we're your neighbor!"

How can a country so large get away with a military that only has fifteen thousand active members? How can you get away with having that small of an army to protect yourself? Is it because you don't step on anybody's toes or piss anybody off? No! Nobody bothers you because you live next door to the meanest bikers in town. Us! And that's the only reason. Look . . . you've been standing in the rain under our umbrella long enough. The time is now to start paying for the protection that *we* provide you.

No more free ride, eh?

Beauty!

Chapter Thirty-eight

AUNT RUTH AND CHANGING TIMES

LONG FOR SIMPLICITY. I'M GLAD THAT I GREW UP IN A rural environment at the very beginning of this technological age that we live in. One of the most poignant moments I remember as a ten-year-old kid was when they came out with Pong, the very first video game. It was Christmas morning when my brother and I were playing Pong and my great-aunt came by to see what we'd gotten for Christmas. She was the same aunt who ran the general store in Sarepta. She sat beside me as I was playing Pong. I noticed tears were running down her face.

"Aunt Ruth? Are you okay? What's wrong?"

She just said, "I'm fine, honey. It just struck me how much smarter you kids are now than we were when I was a kid."

I'm so happy that memory stuck with me. To see those tears, for whatever reason—the gravity of that moment wasn't lost on me as a ten-year-old. I knew something profound had just happened.

When Aunt Ruth was a kid, they didn't have cars or indoor plumbing. No television. She was probably a teenager when radio came along.

The world continues to change at an alarming rate. My kids don't know what it's like to *not* have central heat and air conditioning. They don't know what it's like to have a rotary phone, or a television without a remote control. Back when I was a teenager, I was the remote control in the house.

"Get up and change the channel," my father used to tell me.

I think back to when watching *Gunsmoke* was a weekly ritual in our house. By God, the whole family sat in front of the TV on Saturday night when *Gunsmoke* came on. Those are the bygone days, when the TV stayed on one channel through the whole show. No channel surfing. No picture-in-picture. No multitude of cable channels to bounce back and forth between. We only had three channels: 3, 6, and 12. That was it.

I've decided I've gone as far technologically into the twenty-first century as I choose to go. I don't have a laptop. I don't want one. I don't have a BlackBerry. I don't need that addiction. I don't even have an e-mail address. Don't want one. It's just another way for somebody to pester me. A cellphone's bad enough, but I have one because it would be irresponsible of me as a father not to own one.

I long for a simpler time. Today we sacrifice simplicity for convenience. Unfortunately, if I were dropped into the wilderness, I'd probably be dead in a week. Life is too easy. I can start the morning in Nashville, jump on a plane, and finish my night in Los Angeles without hardly any effort. It's insane. Sometimes I can't help feeling like something's lost. While life is faster and supposedly easier, it's not necessarily a whole lot better. Just like my Aunt Ruth felt.

Chapter Thirty-nine

GETTIN' MY HONKY-TONK FIX

. . .

SONGS ABOUT LOVING AND LIVING
AND GOOD-HEARTED WOMEN, FAMILY, AND GOD.
YEAH, THEY'RE ALL JUST SONGS ABOUT ME.

—from *"Songs About Me"*

N MARCH 2007, "LADIES LOVE COUNTRY BOYS" MADE IT
to number one on the Billboard country charts. We sat on top
for two weeks. It took over twenty weeks to get there because
singles nowadays take an ice age to climb up the charts. But you
know what they say in the music biz? You're only as good as your
last record, so it was especially sweet to score my third number one
as I close in on a dozen years recording for Capitol Records.

Ladies *do* love country boys. Hell, I'm living proof. There's
something about a country boy lifestyle. I'm talking about the *real*
country boys—not the guy who lives outside of town, but the guy
who rides around in a four-wheel drive. Shoots guns. Hauls hay.
Dips snuff. Drinks too much beer. Swings off a rope and swims
naked in the creek. He's the real deal, and women who grow up in
the city are intrigued by that. Especially if they meet the guy and

find out he's not a complete moron, which, unfortunately, is the country boy stereotype. If he's not, then they're *really* intrigued. Whether they'll admit it or not, ladies like that John Wayne type, and the credo the Duke lived by when he said in *The Cowboys*, "I won't be wronged, I won't be insulted, and I won't be laid a hand on."

Or what Tommy Lee Jones as Woodrow Call said in *Lonesome Dove:* "I hate rude behavior in a man. I won't tolerate it."

It's a respect thing. Southern country boys have that crusty, hardcore, living-in-the-dirt side to them, while at the same time there's politeness and good manners instilled from an early age. That's how we grew up. You treat women and your elders with respect. Then you kill everything else that has fur or feathers.

COUNTRY MUSICIANS AREN'T supposed to be competitive. But while we're all buddy-buddy in public, there's an unspoken, underlying code in Nashville: Everybody is supercompetitive. We fake brotherhood; it's actually dog-eat-dog. If it's between me and you for chart position, I want to beat you. That's just how it is.

Nothing is automatic in the music business other than that you have to keep on working through the high times and the lows. But all in all, life in the U.S.A. is sweet. Over the years I've been lucky to have developed a loyal fan base that will buy what I put out and come see me when I come to their towns. Touring and playing are now in my blood. I've always viewed going out on the road as my cattle drive. I'm a cowboy on a cattle drive. I have to get these cows to Abilene, and I'm going to be gone for a while doin' it. But then I get to come back home with a fistful of dollars.

In those early days, I really learned how to tour and play on the road. I still bus it to most all of my gigs. I just have more of them. If it's not over six hundred miles, I'll ride the bus. And that's how I really get to see America.

I carry a seven-piece band so I can play all different kinds of music. When I do traditional country I want to have a fiddle player and a steel guitar onstage. When we play a Southern rock tune, I need two screaming electric guitars. When I do an R&B song, my keyboard player doubles up on saxophone. I have all those musicians available live so the music remains true. One thing is certain: Unless something terrible happens and I don't plan well, I will never go back to just one bus, driving around with a four-piece band again. That ain't gonna happen.

As far as the music goes, I play for the fans. Occasionally along the way, I'll put together a few small venues, like the honky-tonks. I'll tell my booking agent, "Give us a 'tonk' fix so we can see the whites of their eyes." It's like being out on my farm. Every now and then, I need to get gritty and dirty and stinky. I dig that. Maybe it's the heathen in me.

The Rust Belt is one of my favorite touring areas, more specifically the region around Pennsylvania, West Virginia, and Ohio where all the steel mills are. For some reason, Pennsylvania is where I have more members of my fan club per capita than any other state. For a long time, I couldn't figure it out. Then I realized during the time when I was going through my down period, during the dark Garth period, that there was a promoter who ran all county fairs through the Rust Belt. His name is George Moffett from Variety Attractions, based out of Zanesville, Ohio. God bless George. He kept me working through the lean years when I didn't have so many big hits on the radio. By God, he kept me busy on the corndog circuit, and after the years of gigging county fairs, that's turned into one of my strongest grassroots fan bases. Now that we're going great guns, the Rust Belt still draws some of our very best audiences. People there get pumped up and excited. Sometimes we have to call out the riot squad.

In Nashville, we're all cogs in the big music machine. That's okay. Everybody feels that way on the job at one time or another. I don't really want to pull the curtain too far back and reveal what goes on behind this wacky business. Most fans have this vision and idea that the music business is pure. And I don't mean pure in a moral sense, I mean pure in a musical sense, that it's just about music and that we all love music, and that music is Job One, our main priority in Nashville.

But there's more to the business today than music. It's a world-wide corporate thing now, a big-money business, and sometimes I'm just a team member. Labels are controlled by stockholders. Of course there are moments of pure joy in creating music, but those times can be fleeting, so I cherish them. I know a lot of musicians who are all about the business. They're into all the money details and business transactions. I'm not that way. One time I heard Chrissie Hynde of the Pretenders say she's never read a recording contract from front to back because that's not what she's in music for. I'm like her, in that respect. I have people I trust who do that for me. Me, I like playing country music with every kind of spice mixed in.

Call me a dreamer, but at least I keep my dreams in perspective. I dreamed of being a country music star. I knew the odds of it happening were remote, so I didn't put all my eggs in one basket. When I first moved to Nashville, I heard the stories of people willing to give up everything to become a famous singer. Wait tables. Tend bar. Hit all the auditions and songwriter showcases. I got lucky, and despite a few bumps along the way, the road has been relatively smooth and *always* interesting.

There's something to be said for the grit and gravel you gain on the open road, traveling the highways, roads, and boulevards of America. You can't teach five years of playing honky-tonks in college. Nor can you graduate with a music degree and know about playing a club in Texas or dodging a flying beer bottle. I've learned that if you can make folks in a honky-tonk clap and yell for you, then you win. The honky-tonk game was all about survival.

I'm living proof that the American Dream is alive and well. Every day in Nashville, somebody steps off the bus to work at a convenience store in pursuit of that dream, the elusive record deal, the dream that came true for me. I was lucky. Desperation was never my story. Hard work was. Music has always been my love and my life, but never my desperate obsession.

Raising a family and appreciating what a wonderful and free country we live in *has* been my obsession. Like a lot of Americans, I want to do my part to make sure our country stays strong and free, even if it means standing up and saying what might not be popular and politically correct today, but will be true tomorrow. I thank God there are still a lot of reasons to wake up in the morning. Family, friends, and a wonderful country like America to live in. Never a day goes by when I don't thank my lucky stars.

And stripes.

Long may it wave.

—

TRACE ADKINS was born Tracy Darrell Adkins in Springhill, Louisiana. He learned to play guitar at an early age and eventually played with the New Commitments. In the early 1990s he performed solo in honky-tonks, and after gaining some fame he moved to Nashville and signed with Capitol Records. He has released seven albums. His most recent, *Dangerous Man*, debuted at number 1 on the *Billboard* country chart. A member of the Grand Ole Opry, Trace Adkins has appeared on numerous television shows, including *The Tonight Show with Jay Leno, Late Night with Conan O'Brien, Hannity & Colmes,* and *Politically Incorrect with Bill Maher.* He lives in Nashville with his wife and five daughters.

KEITH and KENT ZIMMERMAN are a unique writing team of twin brothers. They are the co-writers of sixteen works, including *Alice Cooper, Golf Monster; Orange County Choppers™: The Tale of the Teutuls;* and *Hell's Angel: The Life and Times of Sonny Barger and the Hell's Angels Motorcycle Club.*

ABOUT THE TYPE

—

THIS BOOK WAS SET in Caslon, a typeface first designed in 1722 by William Caslon. Its widespread use by most English printers in the early eighteenth century soon supplanted the Dutch typefaces that had formerly prevailed. The roman is considered a "workhorse" typeface due to its pleasant, open appearance, while the italic is exceedingly decorative.

03 4014 02241 9437

F
HAR

Hardwick, Mollie

Malice domestic

$13.95

DATE		

DISCARD   DISCARD

© THE BAKER & TAYLOR CO.